Clinical Supervision
A Handbook for Practitioners

Marijane Fall
University of Southern Maine

John M. Sutton, Jr.
University of Southern Maine

Boston   New York   San Francisco
Mexico City   Montreal   Toronto · London   Madrid   Munich   Paris
Hong Kong   Singapore   Tokyo   Cape Town   Sydney

ISBN   0-205-40851-6

Printed in the United States of America

10 9 8 7 6 5 4 3 2   08 07 06 05

Contents

PREFACE

PREFACE

"Supervision contains so many levels of work: There is the client's presentation, the counselor working with the client in relationship, the process of the counseling, the counselor as supervisee in relationship with the supervison, the process of supervision. I love the complexity" (a supervisor).

"Supervision is exciting and energizing to me personally. It is exciting to work as a catalyst for supervisee growth as a professional. I am energized seeing and hearing of the results of that work" (a supervisor).

The supervisors quoted above have one thing in common: They are fascinated by the practice of clinical supervision, the coming together of the art and the science in relationship. Learning about the science of supervision is accomplished through such texts as Bernard and Goodyear's (2004) *Fundamentals of Clinical Supervision*, a compilation of the existing literature that assists the reader with the history, knowledge, and understanding of the skills and practice of supervision. Learning about the art of supervision emerges through the practice of supervision and is the focus of this handbook. Since the art of supervision is difficult to define, we begin with an illustration.

The Case of Deb

Deb arrived at her first individual supervision session for practicum with a high level of anxiety. Her voice was shaky, her thoughts would not materialize, and she exhibited difficulty speaking at times. Despite this anxiety, Deb was determined to succeed in this practicum, where she would be meeting with individual clients.

During her second supervision session, Deb played an audiotape of a counseling session, consisting primarily of the client's voice. Deb's voice was heard only when greeting the client, arranging a second interview, and muttering "oh," "ah," and "um" at infrequent intervals. She focused the supervision session on the issue that she was not "present" during much of the counseling session. She reported struggling with dissociation for two weeks and said that personal medication had been adjusted as a result.

Fifteen weeks later, the supervisor watched this same student work with a client in crisis. Her voice was strong, her speech articulate, and her cognition combined with her emotions in an empathic session that defused a highly volatile client situation.

How did it happen that Deb could become an effective practicum student? It appeared that many factors combined to ensure her success: persistence, openness to supervision, determination, and dogged pursuit of skills. We suspect this is also an example of the art of supervision. Perhaps a listing of supervisor reflections can bring a clue to this elusive definition of "art."

- Where do we draw the line with supervisee mental health issues and counselor training? Do we insist that supervisees suspend practice until all possible symptoms that could affect the client are managed?

- What controls or measures can be in place to assure safety for all persons involved?

- The supervisor reported going by "gut, hopefully combined with experience" in his handling of this issue and others that arose. He questioned whether he could take that chance. When do you act on behalf of the supervisee and supervisee development, and when do you act on behalf of concern for the client?

The supervisor reported that he had worked with the supervisee around the triggering of the dissociation in the counseling session. Cues were discovered, and the student practiced responding to cues prior to dissociation. Since the practicum student was receiving ongoing therapy, the supervisor could assist her by using the language that was already a part of her therapy. The supervisee was able to stay present in the next counseling sessions, although there were short times of inactivity on her part. She demonstrated the use of the learned response to cues preceding dissociation and had no further episodes. She also reported sensing a new control over episodes in all parts of her life and feeling empowered.

The supervisee reported that she had never had such a transforming experience. Her supervisor recognized her disability and through their working together created a relationship that resulted in trust. She stated that she now felt empowered and believed in herself with a new strength. The supervisor reported that he had spent extra hours supervising her, had spent time in his own supervision around his handling of this situation, and had been lucky. He had seen Deb's potential early in the semester, but seldom had he seen such dramatic results by the end of a course.

We believe this was the art of supervision expressed through practice. The supervisor could have asked the supervisee immediately to defer taking practicum for at least a semester. Most of us would have agreed with that decision. Instead, he assessed the situation, decided he could risk the tension, and used the situation to assist the student in building the strength that comes from tackling adversity. They discussed mental health disability issues openly and worked together in a partnership to assist the supervisee. And while he worked for supervisee growth, the supervisor was balancing the necessary assurance of client welfare. He shared that he would not allow most supervisees to proceed in similar circumstances but that he had had a sense that this could be productive. He also knew that at any time he might need to stop the supervisee from continuing and had a contingency plan in place for clients should that occur. The art of supervision was demonstrated in his juggling the tension of risk, excitement, and learning potential for the supervisee with safety for the client and counselor; and this was done with the background of training in the literature, personal knowledge, and skills.

We, the authors, love clinical supervision and are excited to have this opportunity to reach a wider audience for training in the art of supervision. We are dedicated to the belief that supervision is an entity separate from counseling and therefore requires separate training, although it embodies many of the same skills. We feel privileged to have this opportunity to share ideas with you, and we welcome your feedback and commentary on the exercises and information in these pages.

How to Use this Handbook

This book was developed as a companion book to Bernard and Goodyear's (2004) complete compilation of the literature on supervision. It also may be used with other supervision texts, by itself, or in workshops and other training. It contains examples from practice, exercises to assist the new supervisor in determining beliefs, examples of useful tools for supervision, as well as new practice-oriented clinical material. It is our belief that differences in learning styles will dictate how this handbook assists you as a student of supervision or as a professor. Some people may find that the practice-oriented material will help them make meaning of the research and theory. Others will want to start with the literature to develop the necessary background for examining practice. It will be your learning style and preference that will dictate the order.

Overview of the Sections

This book is divided into four sections. Section 1, "The Parameters of Supervision," contains discussion of characteristics of supervision and supervisors, instruments for evaluation of supervision practice, ethical and legal questions for discussion, and examples of management tools such as disclosure statements and intakes. An art needs form, and this section provides some of the practice examples of the structure of supervision.

If Section 1 is the form for the art of supervision, Sections 2 and 3 contain the substance. Section 2, "The Process of Supervision," takes the reader from preparation for the relationship to clinical supervision practice. Section 3, "Supervision Vignettes for Examining Clinical Practice," consists of a series of cases related to the practice of supervision. We conclude with Section 4, "Training," where we provide an outline for an extended workshop in supervision. Combining the science and the art of supervision is an ongoing process of risk taking, development, and practice.

Meet the Authors

Marijane Fall, Ed.D.
Professor of Counselor Education
University of Southern Maine

Marijane Fall is professor and coordinator of the counseling program at the University of Southern Maine in Gorham, Maine. Her undergraduate major was psychology with minors in biology and mathematics. This combination of sciences came together in graduate degrees in counselor education from the University of Southern Maine and the University of Maine. A former elementary school counselor, Marijane focuses her teaching on counseling children in schools, play therapy, counseling adults, and supervision. Her research has centered primarily on counseling children in schools, self-efficacy, and supervision. She has presented at more than 50 national and state conferences, has authored 22 journal articles and book chapters as well as numerous newsletter articles, and has served on national and state committees and boards connected with counseling, play therapy, and supervision. Marijane maintains a small private practice in counseling and supervision.

John M. Sutton, Jr., Ed.D.
Professor of Counselor Education
University of Southern Maine

John (Jack) Sutton is professor of counselor education and chair of the Department of Human Resource Development at the University of Southern Maine. He received his bachelor's degree from Boston College and his master's and doctoral degrees in counseling from the University of Maine. He has taught in the graduate counseling program at the University of Southern Maine for over 25 years. The focus of his teaching is on counseling, mental health, and clinical supervision. His recent academic research and writing have been in clinical supervision and counselor regulation. He is the author of over 25 journal articles and book chapters as well as a variety of other publications and research studies. He has presented at many national and international conferences and workshops over the past 25 years. He has served as president of the Northern New England Association for Counselor Education and Supervision, the North Atlantic Regional Association for Counselor Education and Supervision, and the American Association of State Counseling Boards. He served as a member and chair of the Maine Counselor Licensure Board. He maintains a part-time practice in counseling and supervision.

Acknowledgments

We have chosen to share our brief academic biographies in order that you might understand our backgrounds as supervisors and authors. We also have been and continue to be shaped by our students and supervisees. They have been incorporated throughout this book as reciprocal teachers to us. We would like to express our sincere appreciation to our graduate assistant, Sheila Geant, who has been critical in bringing this book to fruition. She has edited, questioned, and toiled throughout the project. We could always trust she would be one step ahead of us. We owe a debt of gratitude to Janine Bernard and Rod Goodyear for asking us to write this handbook and for their continued support and encouragement. We thank our families and colleagues who have contributed ideas, support, and understanding. This truly has been a collaborative project.

Section 1

THE PARAMETERS OF SUPERVISION

The melding of the art and the science of supervision is represented in clinical practice. This section will focus on (a) descriptions of supervision and your perceptions of yourself in the role of supervisor, (b) characteristics of supervisors, (c) questions to ask when exploring ethical and legal issues and boundaries, (d) evaluation, and (e) tools to manage clinical supervision. Samples of documents are interspersed to serve as guides for supervisors.

Clinical Supervision: What Is It? Who Is the Supervisor?

Determining What Clinical Supervision Is

The word *supervision* has so many meanings that it is confusing when we approach clinical supervision. It seems like supervision is supposed to mean that an experienced person tells other people what is right or wrong with their actions and how to correct them. Parents supervise children, keeping them safe and telling them what to do. Managers supervise employees and tell them what to do and how to do it. Clinical supervision appears to have both similarities to and differences from these commonly accepted meanings.

Metaphors can be used to describe the supervision relationship. Create your own metaphors below.

Metaphors describing the supervisory relationship

Students in an introductory supervision class, such as you may be taking, generated the following list of words related to supervision. How do you see each as related to your role as a supervisor? Are there other words you would use?

Relevant Words	Describe a way you see this concept playing out in supervision.
Support	
Perspective	
Experience	
Growth	
Guidance	
Focus	
Consistency	
Safety	
Spontaneity	
Acceptance	
Encouragement	
Challenge	
Feedback	
Evaluation	
Collaboration	

Based on this list of words from students, what seems to be common are the following constructs: objectivity, evaluation, senior-to-junior status, more experienced to less experienced, development of therapeutic competence, support, educational process, client protection. Here are some reflections on supervision by our supervisees as they discuss why supervision is important.

It is a time to review casework, receive feedback, learn about myself as a counselor, and process my own feelings and reactions so that I am most effective as a clinician.

Supervision means a safe place for me to grow as a counselor. I go to supervision in order to become a better counselor. When I get supervision, that helps me understand my clients, a situation, or a system better. Then I am recharged and hopeful about my work.

Supervision helps me create integrity in my practice. It provides a mechanism to track and explore what is happening to me as I practice as a counselor. Without it, I would not be able to work.

In schools there is so much stress. When I come to supervision it is a place not only to problem solve but also to decompress and process. It is support, an outlet to plug into to recharge my batteries.

The responses below were replies to the question, "How do you benefit from supervision?"

It's a stress reliever. It allows me to be more proactive in what I do as I respond more professionally.

I don't feel so alone.

Preparing for supervision forces me to look at each client and our progress or lack of progress from a different slant.

I can take more risks.

I learn from someone with experience.

I accept my own shortcomings as a professional and then get a chance to really work with my challenges.

Although I am very structured in supervision, sometimes it is just nice to unload to someone who understands a counselor's experience, and then I can work with it.

Group Exercise

Discuss your beliefs about the most important benefits of supervision. When you think about becoming a supervisor, what excites you about it? What concerns do you have?

Characteristics of an Effective Supervisor

You have been examining the meaning and definition of supervision in the previous pages at the same time as you begin to prepare yourself as a clinical supervisor. This section will help you reflect on your level of competence to supervise others. Begin by examining your characteristics as a supervisor and then comparing them with this list.

Standard	I'm OK here	I need more skills/ experience	I have some but need more skills/ knowledge here
Experience as a counselor			
Training as a supervisor			
Effectiveness as a counselor			
Ability to think conceptually			
Ability to manage multiple tasks, relationships, levels			
Awareness of ethical and legal standards			
Multicultural awareness			
Sensitivity to supervisee development			
Ability both to support and challenge			
Ability to be present with a supervisee			

Group Exercise

Discuss your responses to this exercise.

The literature (Gray, Ladany, Walker, & Ancis, 2001; Magnuson, Wilcoxon, & Norem, 2000; Nelson & Friedlander, 2001) suggests that the following supervisor characteristics are not helpful: dismissal and lack of awareness of the trainees' thoughts and feelings, lack of empathy and support, not providing for comfort and/or safety in supervision, all support or all challenge, expression of anger towards the supervisee, moody disposition, unwillingness to share responsibility for supervision, and inappropriate self-disclosure.

Group Exercise

Discuss negative experiences that you have had in supervision and characteristics of supervisors that were not helpful.

An Example of a Supervision Session

The following verbatim transcript is from a supervision session. We include it at this point in the handbook in order that you may gain a sense of the clinical practice of supervision. Some aspects you may want to observe are supervisor and supervisee roles, supervisor focus, and similarities and differences between counseling and supervision.

Supervisee: *Well, I've got two items—a small one I'd like to discuss with you about my notes, and the main thing I want to spend my time on is a client, Tom, about whom I've just briefly spoken to you.*

Supervisor: *It sounds like Tom is a lot more important than your notes.*

Supervisee: *Yes!*

Supervisor: *Why don't we start there, and we'll save some time at the end for your notes.*

Supervisee: *Okay. Let me just refresh you a bit about Tom. He is 71. He requested weekly counseling. He has no goals. He simply wants to come once a week to have a place to talk. He said he picked me because I was a woman, and he wanted to talk to a woman. Because I do work from goals, I worked very, very hard to get some goals from him. And now we've just had our third session last night, and I am no clearer than I was in the beginning. I am clear that he doesn't have a goal; nor does he wish to have one. He has no ways he wishes to be different as a result of working together. I'm kind of stuck about how to work with him.*

Supervisor: *So there is no discernible reason for your meeting. He doesn't seem to want anything. He doesn't want change. He doesn't want your input.*

Supervisee: *He* does *have a reason to meet. He wants to talk to me.*

Supervisor: *But it sounds like you're looking for something different.*

Supervisee: *Counselors have conversations with a purpose. I'm working hard, using my skills, and yet I'm having trouble getting the purpose.*

Supervisor: *I'm a bit confused. On one hand, you say that he doesn't have a purpose, but on the other hand you say that he does have a purpose.*

Supervisee: *Ugh. Not a purpose I want him to have.*

Supervisor: *Oh! All right. Maybe we should start with the purpose you'd like him to have.*

Supervisee: *He appears to be lonely. He has said he wishes to have some social contact, but he doesn't want us to work on that.*

Supervisor: *What's kind of coming across to me is that you have some fairly set ideas about goals. In other words, he's giving you some hints about what most people would look at as goals in terms of wanting social contact. My sense is that he won't go along with you to work on that.*

Supervisee: *I really like him, and perhaps I'm not challenging (that would be the correct word) him as much as I might another client, partly because of his age and situation.*

Supervisor: *So it seems like maybe part of what's happening is that you're seeing him as fragile. How might that be affecting the relationship?*

Supervisee: *It might be facilitating the relationship but not the counseling. When he says he doesn't want to do that, I'm backing off. There's a part of me that really respects what he says. He simply doesn't have the goals I have, and I want to respect that. What I'm having trouble with is the counseling.*

Supervisor: *Something you said intrigues me a bit, and that is how involved you want to be with him. And when I think of that, I think of the word* responsibility.

Supervisee: *By not challenging—it's very possible. There's this piece of me that thinks I would just like to invite him to come to dinner. He's lonely.*

Supervisor: *So listening to you, essentially what you're saying is, "I know what he needs."*

Supervisee: *Oh, I didn't mean that. I'm stuck. That's my question.*

Supervisor: *Yup.*

Supervisee: *I think I do have some ideas of what he needs, but it's not what he's saying. It's only what* I'm *saying.*

Supervisor: *Right. So, what is he saying?*

Supervisee: *He's saying that what he needs is a place to go once a week to talk with a person. He'd like to bring some things in to show me from time to time.*

Supervisor: *Your struggle is that you don't think it's counseling.*

Supervisee: *I feel guilty for taking his money!*

Supervisor: *Not providing a service.*

Supervisee: *Yeah. I'm not providing a counseling service for him. I'm providing a service that he could get at the local YMCA from a volunteer there, and I don't feel good about his paying money for my skills. That's the stuck piece that's in me. He's not dissatisfied. I am.*

Supervisor: *Yes, it sounds like he's pretty happy with the way things are going.*

Supervisee: *I'm dissatisfied because I'm not working as a counselor, although I'm putting more time into my thinking of him.*

Supervisor: *Why do you say you're not working as a counselor?*

Supervisee: *I don't feel that I'm facilitating his moving to a place that is more comfortable.*

Supervisor: *Sounds like that's your definition. Is that his definition?*

Supervisee: *No. You're right. It is my definition. It's like there's a cultural thing here.*

Supervisor: *It sounds like he needs to behave in the way you want him to behave....*

Supervisee: *...to fit my mold!*

Supervisor: *He needs to behave like you want him to behave, and then you'll feel comfortable.*

Supervisee: *Yeah!*

Supervisor: *And he's not doing it!*

Supervisee: *And I feel strange about the label of counseling being put on what goes on at our sessions. I don't mean I'm overstepping the boundaries or anything, but....*

As you read the above transcript, you may have noticed that the dilemma for the supervisor is how to use skills and knowledge to encourage growth without providing answers. The answers are often within the supervisee, and it becomes the supervisor's responsibility to assist the supervisee in accessing them. In other words, the expertise of the supervisor is most often in the use of the skills of supervision rather than in the knowledge of the field of therapy. Although the latter is necessary as background, it is the facilitation of supervisee exploration that maximizes the growth of the supervisee.

Ethical and Legal Questions to Ask Yourself

Supervisors are charged with the responsibility for the development of the supervisee, the treatment of the supervisee's client, and the protection of the public from incompetent practitioners (Bernard & Goodyear, 2004; Bradley & Ladany, 2001; Falvey, 2002; Haynes, Corey, & Moulton, 2003; Stoltenberg, McNeill, & Delworth, 1998). These multiple roles combine with a complex structure that involves a host of rules, regulations, standards, and guidelines. Consequently, there are many ethical and legal standards that apply directly to supervision. Furthermore, supervisors assume a wide range of responsibilities that require in-depth knowledge of the ethical standards of the profession as well as the pertinent laws and legal standards that relate to the professional activities of both the supervisor and the supervisee.

The multiple levels of practice and the complexity of the process of supervision are demonstrated by the following responsibilities held by supervisors. First, supervisors must adhere to all applicable ethical and legal guidelines governing their profession. Second, supervisors assume the responsibility for supervisee compliance with these same ethical and legal standards. Third, supervisors are responsible for instructing supervisees on ethical and legal matters and for monitoring ethical and legal decision making. Fourth, supervisors must behave both ethically and legally in their role as supervisors. These are challenging tasks that no supervisor can take lightly. To meet this challenge, supervisors must be well informed and highly skilled. Following is an outline of a series of questions on ethical and legal issues to assist you as you prepare for your role as a supervisor. We invite you to reflect on them, read about them in texts such as those listed above, and discuss them in groups.

Ethical Questions in Clinical Supervision

Training

What training or qualifications does a supervisor need?

What do professional associations say about training in supervision?

Confidentiality

What are the parameters of confidentiality in the supervisory relationship?

Informed Consent

What information does a supervisee need to disclose to a supervisor?

What information does a supervisor need to disclose to a supervisee?

Professional Development

What is the supervisor's responsibility toward his or her own professional development?

Should supervision count as a professional development activity?

Culture

What is the supervisor's responsibility associated with the supervisee's development of cross-cultural supervision skills?

What is the supervisor's responsibility related to multicultural sensitivity to supervisees and clients?

Crisis Situations

What are the role and responsibility of a supervisor when the supervisee has a crisis event?

Supervisee Impairment

What is the responsibility of the supervisor when the supervisee is impaired and not providing competent services?

Endorsement

What is the obligation of the supervisor in endorsing a supervisee?

Record Keeping

What records is the supervisor responsible for maintaining within the supervisory relationship?

What records is the supervisee responsible for maintaining within the supervisory relationship?

Supervisor of Interns

What are the responsibilities of university faculty and site supervisors for intern placement?

How are the responsibilities of faculty, site supervisor, and intern differentiated?

Evaluation

What is the responsibility of the supervisor for evaluating the supervisee?

How will the supervisee be evaluated?

How often will evaluation take place?

What will be the content of evaluations?

How will the supervisor be evaluated?

Dual Relationships

When are dual relationships in supervision considered unethical?

What are some examples of dual relationships that may be of concern but are manageable?

What are the criteria normally used to evaluate the risks associated with dual relationships?

What are some of the criteria for evaluating the potential for harm to the client?

What are the rules for using counseling with your supervisee?

General Questions Related to Ethics

What is the role of catch-as-catch-can supervision? When is it ethical/unethical?

Should there be a limit on the number of supervisees that a supervisor supervises?

When a supervisor charges a fee for supervision, does this create a dual relationship with the supervisee? Explain.

What are a supervisee's due process rights? To whom does the supervisee complain when there is an unresolved conflict with a supervisor?

What are the implications for the supervisor when complaints are made against the supervisee?

What are the responsibilities of the supervisor related to termination and follow-up for clients?

Key Legal Issues in Clinical Supervision

"Respondent Superior"

> What does this legal principle mean?

> What does this legal principle mean in the context of supervision?

Responsibility

> In supervision, should volunteers be considered the same as employees?

> What are the legal parameters for the site supervisor and the university supervisor when supervising practicum/internship students?

Following are some recommendations that may assist you in protecting clients, supervisees, and yourself from unwanted and unnecessary legal questions:

1. Supervise only in areas of expertise.
2. Choose a specific supervisory model.
3. Avoid/manage dual relationships.
4. Evaluate supervisees on a regular basis.
5. Be available to your supervisees.
6. Formulate a sound contract.
7. Be aware of financial considerations and their consequences.
8. Maintain professional liability insurance coverage.
9. Supervise honestly and with integrity.

Evaluation

Evaluation is considered to be a foundational aspect of clinical supervision, which embodies the supervisor roles of monitoring supervisee development and serving as a gatekeeper for the profession (Bernard & Goodyear, 2004; Bradley & Ladany, 2001; Haynes, Corey, & Moulton, 2003; Stoltenberg, McNeill, & Delworth, 1998). Many supervisors look at evaluation with a love-hate relationship, since it poses some significant challenges. Since most supervisors have been trained as nonevaluative advocates, they often exhibit reluctance, lack of skill, and anxiety in conducting evaluations. These challenges notwithstanding, evaluation is ever present in all stages of supervisee development and cannot be ignored or overlooked.

We provide two different formats for structuring evaluation in supervision. The first is an objective instrument designed for flexibility. It provides structure for both the supervisor and supervisee, who must collaborate on both the evaluation criteria and the scale items. The second format is a subjective written narrative that can provide the supervisee with a different type of data. We recommend that you try out both or use them in combination.

Supervisee Performance Assessment Instrument

The Supervisee Performance Assessment Instrument (SPAI) is a multifaceted tool that allows for self-assessment by the supervisee, collaboration between the supervisor and the supervisee, and/or supervisor assessment. The design of this instrument is to focus on the collaborative process between the supervisor and the supervisee through the option of choosing both the evaluation criteria and the performance scale items. In developing this instrument as a collaboration tool, we decided to depart from many other scales by introducing a large number of evaluation criteria and by using a nonhierarchical type of scaling. Our rationale behind these two ideas is to provide the user with as much flexibility as possible in creating an evaluation tool that meets the needs of both the supervisee and supervisor.

The evaluation criteria of the SPAI are arranged in five categories. These categories consist of skill development, case conceptualization, and personalization as defined by Bernard's (1979) Discrimination Model, with the addition of professional issues and supervision skills. We have attempted to include as many different criteria for assessment in each category as possible, and thus you will find there are far too many for any one situation. This allows the supervisor and supervisee to choose the specific criteria for evaluation and tailor these to specific individuals or groups. This instrument also has the flexibility of accommodating additional criteria to customize the evaluation for individuals or unique applications.

The absence of a traditional evaluation scale is a foundational feature of this instrument. Traditional scales often succumb to response styles such as the halo effect, generosity, and central tendency. We are suggesting the use of some combination of the following instrument scale items.

A. I have not been trained in using this skill.
B. I seldom use this skill.
C. I use this skill often.
D. This is a skill that does not fit my model/style.
E. I am comfortable using this skill.
F. I am uncomfortable using this skill.
G. I would like additional information and training on this skill.

Supervisees may choose one or more of these scale items based on their own self-reflection. This type of scale is far less hierarchical and lends itself to more discussion and action. Although this scale is designed for supervisees, supervisors could adapt it to fit their needs by inserting more hierarchical words, such as *adequate/inadequate, sufficient/insufficient, satisfactory/unsatisfactory, effective/ineffective.*

We describe this as a collaborative instrument. The collaboration takes place between the supervisor and supervisee in developing the specific criteria and scaling to be used in each application. Following is a brief example of this assessment in action.

Example: The supervisor and supervisee collaborate and focus on each of the five categories, together choosing the criteria that best apply to the supervisee's situation. In this example, we have chosen the criterion, "Helps clients build on their strengths." Once the criteria have been identified, the supervisee decides which scale items best describe his or her situation and goals. In this example, the supervisee might pick the following:

B, F, G   Helps clients build on their strengths

Note: B, F, and G represent instrument scale items above. B = I seldom use this skill; F = I am uncomfortable using this skill; G = I would like additional information and training on this skill.

In discussion with the supervisor, the supervisee says that she is not using the skill often because it feels awkward, as though she is praising the client. This dialog both identifies the area of weakness and provides sufficient information to begin forming a plan to increase the efficacy of the behavior.

The SPAI

Place the letter(s) of the instrument scale items chosen in the space preceding the criterion.

Intervention Skills

_____ Listens to verbal and nonverbal communications

_____ Projects warmth, caring, and acceptance

_____ Communicates empathy and genuineness with clients

_____ Communicates effectively, using basic skills such as paraphrases, reflections, questions, and summaries

_____ Establishes effective therapeutic relationships

_____ Observes in-session behavior (e.g., client language) and uses it to facilitate the client/counselor relationship

_____ Uses silence as an effective intervention technique

_____ Times interventions to maximize effectiveness

_____ Attends to the relationship with clients

_____ Demonstrates readiness to explore charged areas

_____ Understands and uses resistance to assist clients

_____ Demonstrates effectiveness in making formal assessments

_____ Performs effective harm assessments

_____ Assists clients in goal setting

_____ Helps clients build on their strengths

_____ Assists clients in assuming responsibility for their progress in therapy

_____ Assists clients in normalizing their behavior

_____ Understands how to help clients change their behavior

_____ Understands how to assist clients who are in crisis

_____ Demonstrates an ability to be concrete and specific

_____ Assists clients in identifying and exploring presenting problems

_____ Demonstrates the use of multiple approaches to treatment

_____ Works effectively with immediacy

_____ Exhibits control of the session

_____ Models effectively for clients

_____ Assists clients by partializing behavior

_____ Effectively uses reinforcement

_____ Rehearses new behaviors and skills with clients

_____ Effectively uses contracts and homework assignments

_____ Makes referrals when necessary

_____ Is knowledgeable about planned breaks, interruptions, and unplanned endings

_____ Is knowledgeable about termination:

    _____ Reviewing the treatment process

    _____ Giving and receiving feedback

    _____ Saying goodbye

Conceptualization Skills

_____ Identifies relevant client themes and patterns
_____ Assists clients in perceiving situations from different points of view
_____ Assists clients in creating new perspectives
_____ Uses client information to develop working hypotheses or hunches
_____ Makes relevant observations about client behavior
_____ Identifies and uses client discrepancies
_____ Perceives underlying client issues
_____ Uses client cultural background in assessment, diagnosis, and treatment
_____ Encourages clients to hypothesize about their own behavior
_____ Assists clients in developing relevant focus and direction
_____ Evaluates the efficacy of interventions
_____ Is knowledgeable about systems and their impact on the client
_____ Accurately ascertains the reality of the client
_____ Adapts theory and techniques to meet the client's reality
_____ Grasps the complexity of issues involved with each client
_____ Willing to reevaluate the conceptualization of the client
Diagnosis and treatment:
_____ Identifies presenting symptoms and formulates DSM diagnoses
_____ Formulates hypotheses based on client information
_____ Develops appropriate strategies and interventions based on established counseling theories and techniques

Personalization Skills

_____ Recognizes personal assets and liabilities
_____ Perceives self in relationship with clients
_____ Directly addresses the relationship process
_____ Understands differences between clients and self
_____ Understands the dynamics of transference and countertransference
_____ Perceives and addresses countertransference
_____ Understands power and influence and their use in enhancing client development
_____ Perceives and understands boundaries in the client/counselor relationship--e.g., limit setting, sexual involvement, time limits, gifts
_____ Sets and maintains appropriate boundaries
_____ Understands the advantages and disadvantages of self-disclosure
_____ Responds effectively to personal questions
_____ Is knowledgeable concerning out-of-office contacts
_____ Works effectively with clients who are culturally different
_____ Is aware of own cultural background and how it may influence the client/ counselor relationship
_____ Is aware of own feelings and uses them in assisting clients

Professional Behavior

_____ Participates in continuing education activities such as supervision, consultation, personal counseling, courses, workshops, teaching, reading, writing

_____ Completes paperwork, such as intakes and case notes, in a concise and timely manner

_____ Communicates written information clearly and effectively

_____ Provides a thoughtful disclosure statement to clients

_____ Communicates orally, clearly and effectively

_____ Respects appointment times with clients and supervisors

_____ Possesses working knowledge of relevant professional literature

_____ Dresses appropriately

_____ Is aware and responsive to relevant ethical standards:

    _____ Is knowledgeable about the profession's primary ethical standards

    _____ Effectively applies ethical standards to practice situation

    _____ Has begun to think ethically

    _____ Seeks consultation on complex ethical situations

_____ Is aware and responsive to relevant legal standards:

    _____ Is knowledgeable concerning laws that pertain to counseling practice

    _____ Applies legal mandates to practice situations

    _____ Seeks consultation on complex legal matters

_____ Makes a conscious effort to improve counseling knowledge and skill

_____ Exhibits willingness to work on personal issues

_____ Exhibits respectful behavior towards clients and peers

_____ Demonstrates an awareness of personal influence and impact on client

Supervision Skills for the Supervisee

_____ Initiates dialog with the supervisor

_____ Arrives prepared at each supervision session

_____ Identifies questions, concerns, and issues relevant to current cases

_____ Creates professional development goals for supervision

_____ Shows interest in learning

_____ Understands and incorporates suggestions

_____ Willing to take risks for learning and identifying troublesome situations

_____ Seeks clarification of unfamiliar situations

_____ Accepts encouragement and constructive criticism

_____ Demonstrates concern and commitment to clients

_____ Actively participates in the supervisory process

_____ Shows willingness to engage in and use role-plays effectively

The criteria that have been developed thus far for the instrument have a bias toward the inexperienced counselor, whether a graduate student or a licensed counselor in the temporary-license category. On the other hand, we have found that the more experienced counselors have discovered the instrument to be helpful in another way. For example, in reviewing the criteria, counselors have commented, "I want to brush up on this skill." In addition, some counselors have combined related items into an area of focus. Others have combined some current criteria with criteria they developed based on their unique situations. The design of the instrument lends itself to the flexibility not only of being able to pick and choose from the available criteria but also of being able to create criteria that are both unique and relevant to the individual. Flexibility and adaptability are the strengths of this instrument, and practitioners are encouraged to use it in ways that will be most helpful in enhancing learning.

Tools such as the SPAI can be used by practicum and internship supervisors, by agency supervisors, and as a tool for self-reflection. A second evaluation tool can take the form of a summative narrative evaluation written by the supervisor at the end of a period of time, centering on the supervisee's goals. We have used this format in supervising professionals in the field.

Examples of Narrative Evaluations

Year-End Review for a Counselor in a School

Supervisee Name: _____

Date: _____

Summative evaluation of supervision for the year ended _____

Number of hours of supervision this year: _____ individual hours

                                                 _____ group hours

Number of total hours of supervision: _____ hours individual supervision

                                                 _____ hours group supervision

During this year you have remained in your position as school counselor at two schools. You have taken the Diagnosis and Treatment planning course and continue to work toward state licensure and registration as a play therapist.

What a year! It has appeared as though your concentration in supervision has been diverted towards political issues at your schools. You have felt a lot of stress in response to these issues, mainly because you have felt as though children were not being served in the best way possible. You have also pushed yourself out on a limb of risk and challenge in response to these situations in order to assist children. This is what I wish to discuss.

The two political situations were ones that would stress any counselor concerned with children in a school. You did not take the less risky road and ignore issues. You thoughtfully came forward and spoke to individuals involved in the issues. You did so with great respect and fairness, being mindful of differing styles and orientations. You also informed administrators of your positions, again while maintaining great respect for others involved. These difficult positions in which you were placed have been arenas for the display of your talents as a negotiator and consultant. While your positions have not necessarily brought the results you would like, your responses should bring you the satisfaction of a job well done.

In the group, you have continued to offer ideas for other members. You are gentle and respectful in your feedback and dialog. I suspect that your ways of speaking to others and your level of expertise were two reasons why your assistance as a supervisor was sought. This recognition of your position within the profession has been a battle within yourself. I suspect that you are on the humble side of winning.

You always appear open to feedback, even when put in a place of defending yourself in school situations. I see the same characteristic in supervision. You may not always agree, but you always listen, take in, and weigh what is said. This means that you are learning and growing in a constant process. Perhaps the only flaw here is that it isn't always easy to remember the positive feedback. You are doing this more often as you recall positive happenings from the weeks before supervision. Your taking responsibility for this beginning to our sessions is another example of your taking responsibility for yourself and what you need.

Your goals this year were as follows:

- To continue to examine and work towards change in response to criticism

- To balance student needs (with their parents and teachers; with behavioral consultant) and priorities, and to allow yourself to breathe

You have handled criticism as you do other professional issues. You carefully consider the situation, and then you are direct and respectful in your response. You have accomplished this in some very difficult political situations over this past year. The second goal has been responded to in a similar way to the first. Your emotional response may not feel like it has changed, but you have learned how to move on from difficult situations. You force yourself to not focus on things you are unable to change once you have done what you personally need to do. This flexibility is a key to good mental health.

Recommendations for the coming year are already in motion. You are ready to look at licensure and the Registered Play Therapist–Supervisor (RPT-S) registration. These two will assist you in preparation of next steps. Other possible directions for supervision and growth consist of taking child-centered play therapy in the spring and doing more taping of sessions for feedback in supervision. (Although you have done this in the present year, we have not had a great deal of time to spend on it.)

It has been a successful year that you have discussed in supervision. You continue to end stronger than you start and to grow in professional ways. I look forward to the next step.

Year-End Review for a Counselor in an Agency

Summary of my perceptions: This year has marked a change in our work together. I have felt that it has been much more intense clinical work with more depth. Perhaps this is partially due to the longer time of each appointment. I suspect it is also due to your progression as a counselor. You demonstrate more awareness of yourself as part of the clinical relationship and how you influence and are influenced in this. In one example, what you bring to supervision for ethical discussions are questions concerning the ethical responsibility or the decision itself. Several years ago you "knew" how to respond to ethical dilemmas or would query, "Should I…?" I also perceive that our relationship is changing, perhaps becoming a safer place to express anything that pertains to our work. I'll be interested to see if this is true in your perception as well.

Past versus present: It was interesting to go back to our first meeting in April five years ago. We discussed note taking, a plan for crisis situations, our plan for supervision, and how to help a client get a job. In our recent session, we discussed how to obtain clarity around the role of clinical supervisor as part of your job description, the effect of the pressures of the agency on you, and client termination. Thus you began five years ago with stage one and two counselor development agenda items due to the newness of your degree and the new questions that arise from that. You end this year with a look at the whole picture and your part in that design. Your development as a counselor is portrayed in those agenda.

In that first year your major issues were coping with the demands of licensure when you had already been a professional for many years, role confusion, pressures on the program, not liking to "push clients," and the dilemma of the medical model versus wellness. The dilemmas presented by these issues are still here. What is different is your knowledge of them and openness to dealing with them, your focus on what you can do, and your ability to adjust despite the belief that this is what is best for all clients.

Over three years ago you mentioned that you "have a preference for spinning in my 'N' and whipping off into action," for cognition versus feelings, and for movement versus stagnation. These preferences probably will always be your strengths. I notice that what you are dealing with more in supervision is how to have them not work against you. This is indicative of the depth of your work in clinical supervision this year.

Looking forward: This year began for us in supervision with problems of near-crisis proportions: new clients, new diagnoses, new problems within the same job but a changed emphasis, and more intense work with fewer individuals. Home visits added to the work. For you this has meant very different problems clinically and challenges from the lack of definition of your jobs for all involved. If there is one certainty, it is that next year may bring new challenges.

Some areas on which you may wish to continue to focus:

Role confusion and clarification. This will probably never end in your present position, as it is constantly evolving and changing. Part of this will be awareness of others' expectations of you and choosing whether *you* wish to take on responsibilities.

Balance between thinking, feelings, and action. You sure love to run with problem solving, a great strength in your position. You have been working on better balance with the other modalities.

Comfort with staying in feelings. This is a personal area where you are fighting old patterns.

Managing Clinical Supervision

The management of clinical supervision provides the foundation for communication, clarifies the parameters of supervision, and indirectly addresses client welfare and supervisee development. This segment looks at the preparation for and the beginning of the supervisory relationship. We begin with suggestions for supervisees as they approach supervision. This is followed by two lists of essential information to be addressed at the beginning of the supervisory relationship. We conclude with examples of a supervision intake and supervisor disclosures.

Choosing a Supervisor

A way to begin to think about managing clinical supervision is to envision what questions supervisees have as they approach the supervision process. Supervisee questions can provide information for supervisors to use in planning for a new supervisory relationship. For example, you may take the first questions on supervisor training and experience and consider how you might provide that information to your supervisee.

Qualifications
- What training and experience has your supervisor had in counseling and supervision?
- What licenses/certifications does this person hold in counseling and supervision?
- Is your supervisor under supervision, or does he or she use a consultant?

Role
- Will your supervisor be assuming an administrative role, a clinical role, or both?
- If your supervisor will be your administrative as well as your clinical supervisor, ask your supervisor to discuss how he or she intends to manage the dual relationship inherent in assuming both roles.

General
- What model or models will be used in supervision?
- What modalities will be used in your supervision?
- How will the confidentiality of information be handled?
- What expectations does your supervisor have for you?
- Is your supervisor available, accessible, able, affordable, and passionate?
- How will conflict be handled?

   Note: One suggestion that we have found useful is to discuss cultural backgrounds. You might ask your supervisor whether this could be explored.

Format
- Will your supervision be individual, group, or triadic?
- If it is triadic or group, who will be the other member(s)?

Goals
- What do you want to learn?
- What are your goals?
- What are the objectives to assist in reaching those goals?

The Information Base

   The literature (Bernard & Goodyear, 2004), as well as our experience as supervisors, informs us of the need to gather and disseminate certain information in the initial phase of a supervisory relationship. The following two lists make up this information base. We encourage you to use this content in creating your own means for gathering and disseminating this essential information.

Information to Be Gathered from the Supervisee

- Demographic information
- Education/training
- Experience in the mental health field
- Previous supervision experiences
- Liability insurance
- Ethical training/code followed
- Previous complaints/legal action
- Theoretical orientation
- Supervisee goals/objectives
- Strengths and weaknesses as a clinician
- Professional development plans
- Description of clients served
- Supervision requirements (e.g., internship, licensure)
- Supervisee personal issues that may affect client treatment
- Supervisee's counseling modality/theoretical orientation

Topics to Be Discussed with the Supervisee

- Purpose of supervision
- Details of where, when, and for how long supervision will take place
- Financial arrangements
- Method and type of evaluation
- Duties and responsibilities of the supervisee and supervisor
- Documentation responsibility of the supervisee and supervisor
- Supervisor's scope of practice
- Supervision model used by supervisor
- Confidentiality
- Ethical and legal considerations
- Supervisee's commitment to follow all pertinent ethical and legal standards
- Process for addressing supervisee complaints
- Emergency and back-up procedures
- Use of supervision modalities (e.g., audio/videotaping)
- Supervision session structure
- Cultural background of the supervisor and supervisee
- Practicing within supervisee's level of competence
- Guidelines for reporting to governmental agencies as required by law
- Complaints and due process rights

Gathering and Disseminating Information

There are many different ways to gather and provide the information listed above. Four ways often mentioned in the literature are supervision intake, supervision plan, supervision contract, and the supervisor's disclosure statement (Bernard & Goodyear, 2004; Bradley & Ladany, 2001; Falvey, 2002; Haynes, Corey, & Moulton, 2003). In addition to these more formal or written methods, supervisors usually gather and provide information verbally. Our preference, which has evolved over the years, is to rely on a written intake and disclosure and use verbal discussion for those topics not covered in the two written documents.

Some supervisors may develop a written plan as a way of formalizing the supervisees' goals and objectives. This can be useful at times when a formal written plan is called for by an outside entity such as a licensing board. Likewise, supervisors may wish to develop a supervision contract as a way of carefully laying out a listing of all the role expectations and functions of the supervisee and the supervisor. These two written documents are viable options for the supervisor.

There is considerable overlap in the content of these four documents. How the content is addressed rests with supervisors, who have the responsibility to assess carefully what will work best for them and their supervisees. In the following pages, we provide examples of an intake and supervision disclosure statements. These written documents are what have worked best for us and our supervisees, and we encourage you to use this information as a means of creating what may work best for you and your supervisees.

Supervisee Intake and Example

Although the literature speaks to the need for an intake for counseling and related professions, this term is seldom used for supervision. A specific form for a supervision intake can provide the supervisor with a quick reference over the course of supervision sessions as well as information about areas to explore in supervision. It also can serve to alert supervisors to potential issues. For example, when a supervisee cannot tell which code of ethics is his or her guide, the supervisor receives important notice of possible concern. The list of information to be gathered from the supervisee on page 22 can be used to construct a supervisee intake that would assist you as a supervisor in your current setting.

An example of a supervisee intake follows.

Supervisee name   _____

Address (home)   _____

                    _____

Address (work)   _____

                    _____

Phone (home)   _____ (work)_____

Please answer all questions that apply to you.

License(s)

    Expiration date(s)

    Supervision requirement

Liability insurance company   Limits of liability

Professional training (include educational background, special training)

Have you had an ethics course or workshop?   If so, when?

What code of ethics is your guide?

Have you ever been charged with an ethical violation? If so, when, and what was the outcome?

Describe your job(s) as a professional counselor. Please include information concerning average number of clients per week and particular populations you may serve.
What is your preferred counseling modality/theory?

Do you receive supervision from another professional? If so, please describe how you envision this working for you.

Supervision, by definition is a planned intervention that occurs over time. How frequently do you wish to have scheduled supervision appointments?

What are your goals for supervision with me at this time?

Do you have any concerns of which I should be aware that might impact your counseling?

Supervisor Disclosure Statement and Examples

Professional disclosure has become an important responsibility for supervisors. Supervision disclosure is discussed fully in current literature, supervision texts, and in the guidelines for the Approved Clinical Supervisor (ACS) credential. A disclosure statement for a practicum class is another type of disclosure that you may wish to consider if you are a member of a graduate faculty or a doctoral student preparing to teach a practicum course. We include two examples of disclosure statements from practicum as well as one from an agency/private practice. In constructing your own disclosure statement, it may be helpful to refer to the list of topics in "Information to Be Gathered from the Supervisee" on page 22 as well as to review the two examples that follow. Some particular items that you may wish to consider are your training and background in supervision, your model of supervision, and the limits of confidentiality.

Example 1.

Disclosure Statement of a Practicum Instructor
University Affiliation
E-mail address
Home (emergencies only) and office telephone numbers

I am excited to be your professor and clinical supervisor during this academic term for practicum class. The following material is designed to conform to best practice standards and ensure that you understand our professional relationship and my background.

I have a doctorate in Counselor Education. I am certified by the National Board for Certified Counselors (NCC), am licensed as a Clinical Professional Counselor (LCPC) and a Mental Health Counselor (LMHC), and am an Approved Clinical Supervisor (ACS) and a registered play therapist and supervisor (RPT-S). I have taken a theory course in supervision, have had two supervised practica in supervision, and have attended related workshops. I have taught supervision courses and have been a workshop presenter for supervision training. My general areas of counseling competence are counseling children, adolescents, and adults for developmental concerns and issues related to loss. I have been counseling for 16 years and supervising counselors for 12 years. While I have a small private practice, my major responsibility is university teaching and research.

Supervision is a process whereby one person is designated to facilitate the professional development and therapeutic competence of another person or persons while safeguarding the clients of the supervisee. I have chosen to conduct my supervision using a model that employs the roles of teacher, counselor, and consultant within a developmental framework. I will utilize the teaching role to assist you in learning a technique or a skill. The counselor role refers to the common therapeutic factors that are used to facilitate your personal growth in treatment-related issues where your specific thoughts or feelings are stimulated by the client and interfere with efficacious treatment. Ethically, I cannot provide therapy for you as part of my supervision. The consultant role is useful for case review and for discussion of areas of uncertainty.

During our supervision session, I will help you to focus on the following areas in counseling: process, personalization, conceptualization, and administration. The process skills comprise counseling techniques. Personalization refers to those aspects of your experience that relate to you as a person, such as transference and counter-transference. Conceptualization focuses on how you think about, plan for, and analyze your cases. The administration function covers all other aspects of counseling such as case notes, ethics, licensure, and business practices. Since you will be taping all your counseling sessions, we will use these tapes for review in supervision sessions. In addition, we will use case note review, role-plays, simulations, and other modalities for our sessions.

Practicum is the first of the steps in the developmental process of learning to counsel. My belief is that this can be accomplished only over time with supervised practice and with student reflection on that practice. Supervision will consist of both weekly peer group and individual supervision. My roles will be of professor, group facilitator, and supervisor. As a professor, I will be a facilitator of your learning to counsel. As a group facilitator, I will attend to the process of the group, keep the group on track, and teach a model of peer group supervision. As your supervisor, I will attend to safeguarding your clients' welfare, assist your professional growth, and serve as a gatekeeper of the profession. Your part in this process will be to counsel clients weekly, to prepare paperwork weekly on all counseling sessions, and to attend weekly supervision sessions and classes. Supervision will require reflection on (1) the counseling process of your client sessions, (2) you as counselor, and (3) the profession of counseling. You will present those issues that remain unresolved at supervision. To this extent, you are in charge of your learning. I will try to help you understand how to prepare for your supervision and to assist peers in peer group supervision.

I will maintain a record of our supervision sessions and suggest that you do the same. Although the records belong to me, they will be available to you to view at any time. I will destroy them one month after your work for the course has concluded.

All information that you share with me concerning your clients or yourself will be kept confidential. There are several important exceptions that pertain to releasing confidential material. I will release confidential material under the following circumstances: (1) You direct me to share information with someone else. (2) I determine that you or a client are a danger to yourself or others. (3) I suspect child, incapacitated person, or elder abuse of you or your client. (4) I am ordered by a court or our laws to disclose information. (5) It is necessary to defend myself against a legal action or formal complaint that you and/or your client make before a court or regulatory board. (6) Your progress requires me to bring your name up before our counseling faculty. In this instance, although I may disclose your client's case or my supervision of you in extreme circumstances, I will not disclose your client's name or other identifying information so that confidentiality may be protected. In addition, I participate both in peer group supervision here at the university and individual supervision outside the university. Your case may be recognized by a faculty member; however, all faculty members attempt to keep the same confidentiality as mentioned above.

My services as your professor and your supervisor will be rendered in a professional manner consistent with accepted ethical standards. Although I am unable to guarantee any specific results regarding your learning goals, we will work together to achieve the best possible results for you. I will assign written work, reading, and viewing of tapes to assist you. I will give you written evaluations at mid-term and at the conclusion of supervision for rating both yourself and me. My belief is that evaluation is an ongoing process that should be as clear as possible. If you are dissatisfied, please let me know. If we are unable to resolve your complaints, you may follow the procedures outlined in your student handbook.

If you need to reach me by phone and are unable to do so, you may leave a message for me, and I will return your call as soon as possible. If you are unable to reach me in an emergency, please contact one of the following faculty members:

(office)   (home)

Dr.

Dr.

If you have any questions, please feel free to ask them at any time.

Example 2.

Disclosure Statement for Clinical Supervision of Counselors in Agencies and Private Practice

University Affiliation
E-mail address
Calling service and office telephone numbers

I am pleased you have selected me as your clinical supervisor and look forward to a productive relationship. This professional disclosure statement is designed to acquaint you with my qualifications as a supervisor, to provide an overview of the supervision process, and to inform you of a number of administrative details.

I hold a master's degree (MS Ed.) and a doctoral degree (Ed.D.) in counseling. I am licensed in this state as a Licensed Clinical Professional Counselor (LCPC). I am certified as a counselor and as an approved clinical supervisor by the National Board of Certified Counselors (NCC), a private national counselor certifying agency.

I have been a clinical supervisor for 25 years and have held a variety of positions in public agencies, private practice, university teaching, and publishing in the counseling field. My training in supervision includes coursework and workshops attended over the past 28 years. In addition, I have designed curricula and taught workshops and courses in clinical supervision. Currently I am a professor of counselor education and have a part-time private practice. The supervision portion of my practice includes individuals and groups. I supervise mental health professionals who treat children, adolescents, and adults. My general areas of competence in counseling include examining issues with relationships, life transitions, and self-direction, including areas of mental illness.

Supervision is a process whereby one person is designated to facilitate the professional development and therapeutic competence of another person or persons. I have chosen to conduct my supervision using a model that employs three roles: teacher, counselor, and consultant. Most often I use the teacher and consultant roles. The counselor role is used at those times when the supervisee's thoughts or feelings are stimulated by the client to the point where they may interfere with the efficacious treatment of the client. However, any intervention will be limited to treatment-related issues, as ethically I cannot provide therapy for you as part of my supervision.

In addition to these roles, I will assist you to focus on the following skill and knowledge areas: process, personal awareness, conceptualizing, and administration. The process skills comprise counseling technique and other essential aspects of the interview process. Personal awareness refers to those aspects of your experience that relate to you as a person and the various influences that occur between counselor and client, and vice versa. Conceptualizing focuses on how you think about, plan for, and analyze your cases. The administration function covers other aspects of counseling from case notes to ethics, and licensure to business practices.

Evaluation is an important and integral part of the supervision process. Evaluation involves making judgments and providing feedback about the quality of work, need for improvement, and the observation of ethical boundaries. We will spend much of our time together focused on your work as a counselor, and my feedback will be ongoing, emphasizing process and progress rather than outcome. At least once a year, there will be a formal, planned evaluation. This evaluation will be based on your goals and other mutually agreed upon criteria. The evaluation will be written and will become part of your administrative file.

I will provide you with the best supervision possible. Our relationship will be professional in nature and built upon mutual respect and trust. My supervision will be consistent with the ethical standards set forth by the Board of Counseling Professionals Licensure. Although the focus of supervision will be on you and your professional development as a counselor, a primary concern will be client care.

I will keep a record of our sessions together. These records will be available to you to view at any time, and I will maintain them for seven years. I suggest that you also maintain your own records. As a supervisee, you are in control of the relationship and may end the supervision at any time, and I will be supportive of your decision.

All information you share with me about your clients or yourself, including any records I may keep, will be kept confidential and will not be shared with others. There are several important exceptions that pertain to the release of confidential information. We both are required to break confidentiality under the following circumstances:

- any threats to harm self or others
- reasonable suspicion of the abuse of a child, elder, or an incapacitated person
- when ordered by the court
- in defense against a legal action or formal complaint made before a court or regulatory board.

You may request that I provide information to others, and I will do so after you have signed a release statement.

In keeping with my own professional development as well as my commitment to effectiveness as a counselor and supervisor, I meet regularly with a counseling supervisor. Although I may discuss your client's case or my supervision of you, I will not disclose your client's name, your name, or other identifying information so that the confidentiality of all parties will be protected.

My fee is $ ____ per supervision hour. The fee is due at the conclusion of each session. Cash or personal checks are acceptable for payment. I will provide you with a receipt for all fees paid. In the event you are unable to keep an appointment, please notify me 24 hours in advance.

My normal appointment day is Thursday. I usually schedule appointments from 8 a.m. through 8 p.m. Appointments on other days will not be readily available but may be scheduled in an emergency. If you need to reach me by phone, please call _____ or _____. If you are unable to reach me at either number, you may leave a message for me, and I will return your call as soon as possible. If you have an emergency and cannot reach me, please call one of the following individuals:

Dr.

Dr.

Dr.

If at any time you are dissatisfied with my services, please let me know. If I am unable to resolve your concerns, you may report your complaints to:

Board of Counseling Professionals Licensure
Department of Professional and Financial Regulation
Division of Licensing and Enforcement
Address
Telephone Number

If you have any questions concerning what is contained in this statement or on other matters related to your supervision, please feel free to raise them at any time.

Please sign and date this form.

_____   _____

_____   _____
              (Date)   (Date)

Supervisor Case Note and Examples

The information that is gathered from the supervisee in such documents as supervision intake, supervision plan, supervision contract, and supervisor disclosure statement becomes the beginning of the supervisee records. Case notes form the continuing documentation of the supervision. Although the literature includes many options for structuring case notes (see Bernard & Goodyear, 2004), we noted an absence of examples. We include two examples, one from a supervision session with a supervisee in practicum and the second from a session with a supervisee who is an advanced clinician. You will see the difference in attention to detail of paperwork, audio/videotape, and verbatim. We list the supervisee's presenting problem, issue, or question and how we dealt with it within the supervisory session. If ethical issues are discussed, we note those separately. As you look over these examples, you may want to pick out features that would fit your needs as a supervisor.

Example 1. The following sample of notes is from a supervisor of a practicum student. The supervisor keeps track of all clients. This student has been trained to arrive at supervision with an agenda, which is written at the top of the note. This helps the supervisor manage the time available. The supervisor generally reads the case note for every client every week, reviews required transcripts, and listens to tapes for most but not all client sessions. In this example, the supervisor did not listen to the audiotape of the first client, since the focus was on the supervisee's feelings. With the second client, the supervisor watched the video and reviewed the transcript. The informal note taking or paperwork and tapes help the supervisor keep track of how cases have been reviewed with the supervisee. It also allows the supervisor to keep track of assignments (e.g., transcripts). You will notice that this case note is brief and objective and uses phrases more than sentences. Although not reflected in this example, special notations that may represent areas of concern, patterns, or other noteworthy points are often made by the supervisor.

(Name of Supervisee)   Date:

Agenda
      Review two cases
      Two administrative questions
      Supervisor agenda item

Question: Do I call her?	(Client's name) Case Note Supervisee's client cancelled and has not rescheduled. Supervisee has seen her for ten sessions and reports client has made significant progress. Supervisee feels stuck between sadness and accomplishment. Discussed: Supervisee's feeling of sadness as it relates to client and feeling of loss. Supervisee decides not to call; will wait for client to call.
Question: This occurred a long time ago. Do I have to notify the state authorities?	(Client's name) Case note/videotape/transcript Supervisee's client reported being abused by a family friend 30 years ago when she was a teenager. Supervisee is reluctant to report, worried about the impact on the relationship. Watched video and reviewed transcript of supervisee responding to client reporting abuse. Client aware of supervisee's obligation to report via disclosure statement. Supervisee directed to report.
Questions: I can't get my clients to set goals and need help. How can we set goals when they say they don't have any?	(Client's name) Supervisee gave several examples. Assisted the supervisee in looking at the problem from a different direction. In viewing the problem differently, supervisee came up with some new ideas. We will discuss again next week.
I am not sure I am doing my case notes properly.	Explored supervisee's concerns. Reviewed several current case notes. Discussed purpose of notes. Supported supervisee in developing own style.
Supervisor's agenda:	Supervisee did not do a harm assessment with (client name) during intake. Supervisee expressed fear that to do so would harm the relationship.
Discussed:	Supervisee directed to perform harm assessment at next appointment. Explored ways of minimizing impact on the relationship.

Example 2. The following sample of notes is from a supervision session with L. She is an experienced and fully licensed counselor. The supervisor does not keep track of L's clients with the exception of at-risk cases of clients that she identifies. The supervisor can trust that L will bring issues with clients to supervision at appropriate times. She prepares the agenda and always begins with affirmations, listing what she feels good about. In the past, she identified this feature as necessary for a forced reflection, as her job does not lend itself to positive evaluation or feedback. Although L's focus is on what she needs to improve, she is cognizant that she needs to affirm herself as well.

Notes from (date)
Session 21
1-hour individual supervision
Paid in full

Supervisee's agenda items

Affirmations:	Two clients terminated, having made many positive changes. Tried intervention rehearsed in supervision – successful. Began new course at university.
Question:	I had a new client, did a 1.5-hour intake, and haven't seen client since. I know this happens but wonder whether I could do things a bit differently. This has happened several times before.
Resolution:	Discussed intake process and identified area of concern – not giving the new client what the client was asking for. (L believes in assisting client to come up with client's own solution and would reflect this to client when client asked for direction within the intake.) After a discussion, we identified a general way to assist a client and used two role-plays of such a situation. First I modeled a counselor role, and L played the client who had recently asked for direction during an intake. We then reversed roles; L was the counselor, and I was a different client. We discussed these interactions, and I gave L feedback on how I felt as a client. L reported that it was helpful.
Question:	Would you look at my intake form for adult clients? I have recently revised it to meet more closely my purposes for information.

Resolution: We explored her purpose for the instrument and checked to see whether her needs were being met by the present instrument. She will share a copy of her revised intake with me at the next session.

Section 2

THE PROCESS OF SUPERVISION

The ongoing course of clinical supervision is complex and ever evolving. This section will illustrate that intricacy and movement. We begin with a transcript of the opening of a supervision session, illustrating central concepts and ideas for practice. The first topic, "Supervision Tasks and Process," discusses training the supervisee in preparing for supervision. This is followed by supervisor preparation, a discussion of relationship variables and roles, interactive vehicles for expanding a repertoire of responses, and a checklist for getting started. Practice examples with our commentary point out facilitative and nonfacilitative responses of a supervisor. We then invite the supervisor to go beyond cognitive communication with the use of such creative mediums as sandtray and artwork in both individual and group formats. The section concludes with a series of topical problems and suggestions that new supervisors may find helpful when beginning the practice of clinical supervision. The section contains many foci, much as supervision itself presents a kaleidoscope of images, all rotating in relation to each other.

Transcript of the Beginning of a Clinical Supervision Session

As we discuss the process of supervision, it is helpful to have a picture of the supervisor and supervisee in relationship in an actual session. We include this transcript of the beginning of a session so that you can visualize the direction of our training. As you read the transcript, notice the preparation of the supervisee as well as the supervisor's focus on the supervisee. It is the supervisor's focus that is the concept of "thinking like a supervisor." The supervisor does not play the expert by providing answers but instead uses his expertise in facilitating the supervisee's search for her own solutions.

The following transcripts of what not to do and what to do in a supervision session were taken from a supervision workshop demonstration. After the second demonstration, we invited the workshop participants to discuss what they had observed.

Demonstration of What Not to Do

Supervisee: *Thank goodness I'm coming to supervision today! Oh man, I need to sit down, get away from that place, and just sit back a bit and talk with you.*

Supervisor: *What do you have that book for?*

Supervisee: *Just some stuff. So how was your Christmas?*

Supervisor: *Great, great. How about yours?*

Supervisee: *Thank God we had a little break. It was good to get away.*

Supervisor: *Good.*

Supervisee: *Did you get any cross-country skiing in?*

Supervisor: *No. I got some sailing in though.*

Supervisee: *No kidding! I hope you went somewhere!*

Supervisor: *Ha ha! Well, let's get started.*

Supervisee: *Well, I haven't really got anything to talk about. I need a break. I need to come here and not think about that place anymore and just shoot the breeze for a bit. That's just what I need.*

Supervisor: *OK, well let's shoot the breeze then.*

Supervisee: *All right.*

Comment: This is not what we consider supervision. It is a demonstration of what not to do. One of the things you noticed is that the supervisee came in without an agenda—well, she had an agenda; she just didn't want to do anything. That's not the way we like supervisees to arrive at supervision. We want them to have an agenda. We hope you will be empowered to change the course of action when your supervisee comes in and just wants a break. One of the ways we do that is preventive, by teaching supervisees how to prepare and how to come to supervision. In addition, the supervisor collaborated with the supervisee in avoiding supervision. He chose to continue to banter with her and to engage in a conversation. Without focusing on the supervisee as a therapist, there is little chance that any supervision will occur.

Demonstration of What to Do

Supervisee: *Oh boy, I'm really glad to come to supervision today. I've been waiting for this. It's been two weeks. I have three things for sure.*

Supervisor: *Okay.*

Supervisee: *One of the things is that when I was in graduate school 20 years ago, they weren't telling us we had to take notes. School counselors weren't taking and keeping notes, not in that way. And also it's just dawning on me that people are talking about all school counselors taking notes, and I wanted to talk about that a little bit because I haven't been keeping notes. What should I keep?*

Supervisor: *That's one agenda item.*

Supervisee: *Probably the biggest thing is I need to talk about is something that's going on at the high school. Something has started with the students. I've heard it now three times, where students are saying they're combining certain drugs and using this for girls to abort pregnancies. That's coming into my office, and I'm having a real problem around that, so I want us to spend most of our time there.*

Supervisor: *And the third agenda item?*

Supervisee: *Well, the pregnancy issue is probably the most important thing, and I do need to check on those notes.*

Supervisor: *Okay, so where would you like to start?*

Supervisee: *Let's do the pregnancy issue, and probably we'll only need five or ten minutes for the notes.*

Supervisor: *All right. So we'll organize our time so that we leave at least five but hopefully ten minutes.*

Supervisee: *Let me tell you a little more about what's happening, and then we'll try to get to what my concerns are around it. And I don't know all of them, which is why I'm here. Recently students have been talking about combining certain drugs. Some of them are prescription drugs, and some are street drugs. They are saying the combination is successful in aborting pregnancies. One student came to me directly and spoke to me about it, and I have heard about two more cases indirectly.*

Supervisor: *Talk about your concerns.*

Supervisee: *Oh boy. There's the ethical piece. Their parents don't know about this, and I know I don't have to tell their parents, but I want them to tell their parents. There's part of me that's scared. What else might this combination of drugs be doing to them? I don't know that, and that's sitting there. I'm worried about the girls physically. And then there's the much bigger thing about the whole school.*

Supervisor: *So we have the ethical piece and whether you should notify the parents or not....*

Supervisee: *There's something really unsafe here that's going to happen later. I know they've already experienced it, but I'm feeling like maybe something else is going to happen, and I'm holding a powder keg. Then there's the education of our student body. I'm scared about kids doing this.*

Supervisor: *Okay.*

Supervisee: *Then there's me. I don't like this. I'm really scared about it.*

Supervisor: *So we have the ethics, the education, and you.*

Supervisee: *Yeah. The worst part is me.*

Supervisor: *Why don't we focus there.*

Supervisee: *I don't feel all right about this happening. It's true that it isn't something that is part of my organized religion. As far as I go, I think I'm kind of breaching that. I'm generally all right with abortion. This is very different. It's not safe, and I feel like I have this knowledge that nobody else has, and it's possibly knowledge of something that's really unsafe, and it's being spread among the student body. I know something that I don't want to know. I'm scared for the kids. I'm holding it; I'm not letting it go.*

Supervisor: *So help me see where you see your struggle with this. You talk about holding this knowledge.*

Supervisee: *A piece of it is right there: holding it and no one else knowing about it. It feels dangerous to me. I feel like the unknown piece of what harm could be coming to those girls could be very dangerous, and I'm holding it.*

Supervisor: *So it's kind of like a big, heavy weight. I have this important, somewhat secret information. What do I do with it?*

Supervisee: *Yeah. I've been a counselor a long time, and pretty much when I close my office door and go home, it stays there until I return the next morning with a few exceptions. This is not staying in my office. I'm lugging it around with me, and I want it lighter. I'm telling you about it....*

Supervisor: *You'd kind of like me to...*

Supervisee: *Take it if you want!*

Supervisor: *In a sense that's part of what you're doing with me. You are sharing that with me.*

Supervisee: *Does that scare you? As I tell you that, does it scare you?*

Supervisor: *What about that scare concerns you?*

Supervisee: *I'm scared for the girls. It's about combining these drugs, and I have this part of me that says, yeah, there was a result, the abortion, but that's really not even where my fear is. My fear is, what else? What else did this combination of drugs do to them? I feel like it's a time bomb, and I'm scared about going into school one of these days and finding out some really bad stuff.*

Supervisor: *What are you scared about for yourself?*

Supervisee: *Well, I guess maybe there are two pieces to that. One would be my tending to my ethical responsibilities, and I want to make sure we look at that.*

Supervisor: *Sure.*

Supervisee: *You might say this isn't myself, but I'm really scared about finding out these girls have been harmed. You know, I like everything to be smooth and nice and to all work out.*

This concludes the demonstration.

A summary discussion follows.

Marijane and Jack = workshop leaders
SIT = supervisors in training

Marijane: *What did you think (addressed to supervisors in training)?*

SIT 1:   *Jack was focused on you, Marijane, and how this problem impacted you, trying to get you to talk more about that and the conflict that was going on inside you and what your fears were.*

SIT 2:   *Jack, there were several times where you could have gone into a problem-solving mode with her, and you didn't. You stayed with her where she was.*

Jack: *Let me talk a bit about that because there are times when I do go into a problem-solving mode. But what I find is that the longer I can hang out, the more initial issues fall by the wayside, and we get down to some of the core concerns. And when we get down to something that is really core, often that illuminates some other issues, and we can move quickly by those. If I had grabbed onto that ethics piece—and that's always a temptation for me—I'd have missed out on the core of the issue.*

SIT 3:   *Do you imagine that you would eventually have some discussion about lugging the burden around?*

Marijane: *If we need it, but I think what Jack is saying is that by hanging in there with me, we may not even need to go there because as it gets cleared up for me, I may know how to solve the problem without his help.*

Jack: *I opened a little bit of a door when I said that sharing with me was a way to get.... That opened a bit of a door. I might not have to say anything more about that because she may come back at some later point in the session and say, "It was important for me to talk about that, and maybe I need to talk to some other people." So she can set up her own plan like that.*

Marijane: *And then if you think about one of our roles of being a supervisor, the major focus is to assist with our supervisees' growth. So it's much more important that supervisees work to get there than that we tell them how to get there.*

SIT 4:   *Jack, the thing I really liked is that in the beginning, you asked what she had, but instead of really accepting what she was saying about doing 14 minutes here and 15 minutes there, you really let her hone the point on the issue. And instead of just saying, "It sounds like you have an issue with this," you kept putting it back to her to keep sharpening and simplifying.*

Marijane: *And that's very empowering for the supervisee. That's like we're working together, but I'm in control, and that's helpful for me as a supervisee.*

SIT 5:   *But, Jack, even though you kept throwing it back to Marijane, you kept saying, "We have this to work with and this to work with, etc." So you still brought some structure to what she needed to take care of.*

This concludes the discussion.

Supervision Tasks and Process

Preparation for the Supervisee

Well-trained supervisees make us look good as supervisors! We suspect that this was evident to you as you read the preceding transcript. The supervisee arrived with a prioritized agenda of what she wanted to get from supervision that day. We believe this is so important that we begin our section on the supervisor tasks and process with training for the supervisee. Following is a document that can be copied and handed to supervisees prior to the first meeting. It will help to explain the phases of supervision and supervisee preparation.

Phases and Structure of a Clinical Supervision Session

It may be helpful to think of each supervision session as having three separate phases. Not participating in any one phase detracts from the impact of the supervision experience in its entirety.

Phase 1: Advanced Preparation

We consider this phase to be the most important, since it determines how much one gains from a supervision session. The following questions provide structure that leads us through the preparation process.

What will you bring up in supervision? Examples of content and process follow.

   A. Content
- Introducing new cases
- Reviewing previously discussed cases
- Personal awareness
- Reviewing administrative issues
- Evaluation
- Cultural influences

- Crisis issues
- Ethical and legal issues
- Professional development

B. Process: It is the supervisee's responsibility to construct the supervision agenda. Supervisees are the architects of their own learning and need to be proactive, assertive, and, most importantly, courageous in reflecting on themselves, their clients, and their behavior as counselors/therapists. In the reflection process, there are a number of focus points and questions to consider.

- Counseling Technique Dilemmas

  What are you doing to assist the client? How is it helping? Where are you stuck? What ideas do you have about helping your client? What is stopping you from trying out your ideas? How could you behave differently?

- Client Problems

  What puzzles you about your client? What would you like to know about his or her problem? How could you find out what you don't know? What resources do you need?

- Personal Issues

  What is happening to you in this situation? How are you feeling? How are these feelings influencing your counseling? What is your purpose? How is your counseling behavior related to assisting your client? What are your hypotheses about your own behavior? What needs to happen for you to behave differently?

- Administrative Questions

  What are the ethical/legal issues involved with this client? What assistance do you need with maintaining your professional qualifications and development?

- Treatment Planning/Action Issues

  What are your client's symptoms/problems? What hypotheses do you have about your client and/or your client's behavior? What meaning do your client's situation/personal issues have for treatment? What are the counselor's goals, and are they separate from the client's goals? In what stage of change is the client? What treatment modalities/interventions will be used? What additional resources are necessary?

- Unresolved Issues

  What are the multicultural issues between you and the client? Between you and your supervisor? How will you address these issues? What disagreements do you have with your supervisor? How will you handle these disagreements? Have you asked how your supervisor would like you to implement his or her suggestions?

1. What is the priority for your supervision topics?

2. What do you need from your supervisor around each topic?

3. How will you present this topic to your supervisor (i.e., what modality will you use)? Examples of modalities are self-report, audio/video recording, case note review, observation, co-counseling, live supervision, role-play, telephone conversation, and supervision via computer technology. It is important to use differing modalities for supervision learning and for you to get the most from your time with your supervisor.

Phase 2: Supervision Session

This is your actual supervision session. You present your supervisor with your agenda. You control the session to the extent that you need to make sure that you get your needs met. It is helpful to share your proposed agenda with the supervisor at the beginning of the session. Then, as you proceed to each topic, explain what it is that you need from supervision. At the same time, it will be important to take notes of the session so that discussions and decisions will be easily translated to new counseling behaviors.

Phase 3: Translation of Ideas into Action

You leave supervision. What is your plan for translating your notes into action? How will you incorporate this new learning into your counseling sessions?

Preparation for the Supervisor

We begin this section with an overview of the supervision process. A more specific focus on relationship and role follows from a transcript and discussion.

Session Structure

Well-prepared supervisees deserve well-prepared supervisors. Supervisees have provided us with feedback that in order to have a vision of the process, they need concrete and specific information. In response, we formulated the list below to inform supervisees of the nuts and bolts of a supervision session.

- Give the "Phases and Structure of a Clinical Supervision Session" document to the supervisee. (See page 41.)

- Have the supervisee arrive at supervision with a prioritized agenda.

- As each agenda item is introduced, help the supervisee clarify what the issue is and how you, the supervisor, can help. This exploration often results in an unfolding process that may lead in unanticipated directions. Typical questions that may be asked by the supervisor are listed on the supervisee's handout. For example:

  > What is confusing to you about this case?
  > What would you like to happen as the result of our discussion?
  > What puzzles you about this client?

- What will be the focus for supervision?

  > Skill development?
  > Case conceptualization?
  > Personal awareness?
  > Professional behavior?

- What role will you use?

  > Teaching?
  > Counseling?
  > Consulting?

- Check and recheck with the supervisee. For example:

  > Did you get what you need?
  > Are we finished with this?
  > Have we covered this enough?

Supervisory Relationship

The supervisor/supervisee relationship is considered to be a critical variable in the overall success of supervision (Bernard & Goodyear, 2004). The responsibility for the quality of this relationship is weighted toward the supervisor. There are a number of factors that you may want to consider as you enter the role of supervisor. Following are some suggestions we have found helpful in structuring an effective supervisory relationship.

1. Establish clear written goals.
2. Discuss the roles of both supervisor and supervisee, including the supervisor's model of supervision.
3. Disclose to the supervisee what the process of supervision will be like as well as the supervisor's expectations.
4. Communicate to the supervisee the evaluation process, including expectations, timing, and criteria to be used.
5. Establish a process to resolve conflict.
6. Establish a process for ongoing feedback apart from any formal evaluations.
7. Respect the supervisee while offering constructive criticism about behaviors.
8. Maintain professional boundaries.
9. Discuss ambiguity that may occur as a result of encouragement to explore limitations while at the same time being evaluated for suitability for the profession.
10. Acknowledge supervisee anxiety, and identify the sources of the anxiety.
11. Create an atmosphere in which support and challenge coexist.
12. Use communication techniques such as metaphors, analogies, and humor.
13. Encourage a more egalitarian relationship through collaboration.
14. Monitor the relationship itself through the use of immediacy.
15. Be fully present with the supervisee.

In addition to the list above, supervisors' feelings can be used as clues to the dynamics of the supervisor/supervisee relationship and to initiate interventions designed to further the development of the supervisee. Following are common feelings that counselors often encounter in their work with clients:

frustration	boredom
anger	rage
confusion	alienation
sympathy	protectiveness
anxiety	fear

These feelings may provide important clues to how the supervisee is responding to and treating clients. The supervisor can use the knowledge gained from these feelings to provide more effective feedback to supervisees.

We have suggested many tools for you to use as you are learning this new material. The tools provide the framework for the literature foundation. We are aware that the heart of the art of supervision defies words, and yet it is the essence of the relationship. We can be good supervisors without it, forming questions to assist our supervisees and gaining direction from the unexpressed and expressed meaning and feeling emanating from the supervisee. However, we suspect that there is another element present in great supervisors. They are able to combine the characteristics of a good supervisor with an ability to work within the relationship at that moment, with all that is past and present. We have no listing of steps or questions for you to work through to get there. Great supervision is the art of the relationship, and the development of the relationship is a function of practice.

What Role Will You Choose?

One way to begin to think like a supervisor is to expand awareness of possibilities of supervisor responses and to practice responding. The transcription below creates such an opportunity. In a clinical supervision workshop, we, Jack and Marijane, begin a supervision session with Jack as the supervisee and Marijane as the supervisor. After the first few transactions, we stop and invite workshop participants (trainees) to share possibilities for the next supervisor intervention. The responses from the trainees along with the rich discussion allow for further expansion of the trainees' thinking. We have found this demonstration format to be an invaluable instructional technique in training supervisors. It provides both a safety net for trying out new behaviors and an opportunity to develop the conceptual thinking necessary to be an effective supervisor. As you read this section, you may want to formulate your own interventions, choosing the role of teacher, counselor, or consultant.

*****

Marijane: *Hi.*

Jack: *Marijane, as you know, some of the work I do is in a hospital. I had a situation the other day that I can't get rid of, and I'm really struggling with it. I'll tell you what happened. I received a call to come in and spend some time counseling a patient in the hospital who was dying, was really quite ill. It was an emergency. I got beeped, so I immediately went to the hospital. When I got up to the room, the family was there but left the room, saying, "He wants to talk to you and only you, so we'll be outside." I had seen him twice before, so I had a relationship with him. He had deteriorated since the last time I had seen him. He started to talk to me, but*

I couldn't understand him. He could not articulate his words to the point where I could comprehend them. I didn't know what to do. One of my first thoughts was, "I'll get a piece of paper." He tried to write, but he didn't have enough physical control of his hand. He could not write. He became more and more frustrated, and of course I was feeling terrible. I had come in knowing he wanted to talk to me and that he didn't want to say anything to his family about what he wanted to tell me. I figured he only had a little time left to live, and he really wanted to get something off his chest, but as hard and as often as I tried, I just couldn't understand him. I just can't let go of that.

Marijane: *So it's still with you.*

Jack: *Absolutely, absolutely. It's still with me, and I can't get over the real pain I felt because I could not understand him.*

Supervision session ends temporarily.

Marijane: *Where might I go with him next, choosing the role of teacher, counselor, or consultant?*

SIT 1:   *I'd go with pain, the pain he felt, and I'd use the supervision role of the counselor.*

SIT 2:   *I'm thinking I would be in the counselor role too because it seems that something has been triggered within the supervisee. Anyone who couldn't understand someone would feel awful, especially if you were the one person he wanted to talk to, but it also seems like there's something in the supervisee. I might do some reflecting back.*

Marijane: *So what would you say?*

SIT 2:   *"It sounds like you're in a tremendous amount of pain. Would you like to say more about that?"*

SIT 3:   *I personally would go not very deep, but I would go into the counselor role and explore and help him let go of those feelings a little bit.*

Marijane: *So what would you say?*

SIT 3:   *I'd probably say, "It sounds like a lot of weight was put on your shoulders when the family said he only wanted to speak to you, and you've been put in this dilemma of the client not being able to speak to you. I'd like to just speak to that and have you talk to me a little about how that's making you feel because it sounds like you can't let go of that and that it's been haunting you."*

SIT 4:   *I prefer the counselor role as well. I would just reflect, "It looks like you're in a lot of pain around this." I'd start to try to bring closure to that.*

SIT 5:   *I am wondering whether it's okay to ask for clarification about interventions by saying, "Is that what you want to talk about today?" Should we set the agenda like you role-modeled earlier by saying, "I hear you're in a lot of pain. Is that what you want to talk about?"*

Marijane: *Yes. I would like to see where he wants us to go with that. I do want to reflect where he is, but I'm also very aware that he could say to me, "I've just got to talk this out with someone. I've been holding it. I haven't been able to talk it out." He might say, "Whoa, this has really triggered something inside me, and I'd like us to work on that." I want him to decide.*

Return to supervision session.

Marijane: *It sounds like that's a really heavy burden you're still carrying. What I'd like to know is what you'd like from me or from our working together.*

Jack: *I don't know. I don't really know. I know the feelings I have. I know I need to talk about this, but I really don't have a handle on what the question is.*

Marijane: *Listening to you, I hear your frustration with this. I'm hearing how you're still holding it and what it was like to have this handed to you, that he really wanted to talk to you, and you couldn't understand him. I'm also hearing that you really want to talk about "this," and I'm not quite sure what "this" is. Where would you like us to start?*

Jack: *I don't know whether I know enough right now where to start.*

Marijane: *Yes.*

Jack: *I think it really has a lot to do with how I'm feeling. There's a lot of frustration around what I was unable to do. I couldn't listen, and that's one of the things I'm trained to do.*

Marijane: *You couldn't do it.*

Jack: *I could listen, but I couldn't hear.*

Supervision session ends temporarily.

SIT 1:   *I think it's time to move to a consulting mode, and I think he has a real need to go through this process.*

SIT 2:   *I think that could be important, so I'd be interested to know how he feels about not being able to listen or hear and what he thinks about all this.*

Marijane: *You're talking about consultation and sitting with him as he explores this and trying to help him examine this. I'm probably still there. He hasn't given me direction, but he wants to be into it, so I want to allow him to keep going further. He's still struggling with what it is he needs and why he's holding all of this, and I don't know why he's holding on to this.*

Return to supervision session.

Marijane: *You listened, but you didn't hear.*

Jack: *That's right. I listened, but I didn't hear, and that was very frustrating because what happened was that he was very aware that I couldn't understand what the heck he was saying. Very aware. So he became more frustrated and agitated. So not only was I unable to understand him, but I had a highly agitated dying man in front me...*

Marijane: *...who had selected you to listen.*

Jack: *Yes. Something had happened early in our first couple of meetings, and we made a connection. I felt that.*

Marijane: *And now he needed to be heard.*

Jack: *And now he needed to be heard, and I couldn't do it. I couldn't hear him.*

Marijane: *You were there.*

Jack: *Yup.*

Marijane: *You tried, but you couldn't do it.*

Jack: *Yup.*

Supervision session ends temporarily.

SIT 1: *It sounds to me like there could be an opportunity for some—I'm not sure whether it's consultation or teaching—to the effect that sometimes we can't do what we want to do, and things are out of our control. I think there's an opportunity here to get that in. Would that be teaching or consultation?*

SIT 2: *Well, it's kind of a carryover. It's some validation or counseling, moving into a teaching. It's almost like a transfer so that you can move more into teaching.*

SIT 3: *It seems to me we are all jousting in the dark pretty heavily here. We're doing a lot of overthinking about something when we're supposed to be there with the client.*

Marijane: *Ah! So how do we get there? We might go to helping him put himself back in that moment and to touch into his feelings about it.*

SIT 4: *What's coming up for me is the parallel process between me as the supervisor, trying to get the dying man who can't express himself to talk to me. So with that set up and parallel, I would be tempted to offer the supervisee a means to get really focused on what it is he's trying to say.*

Marijane: *So what would you say to the supervisee?*

SIT 4: *I would ask if he'd like to explore a little bit more because he keeps going back there. We've tried a couple of things to give him an out, but he just keeps going back in. So I'm sensing that there's something important.*

Return to supervision session.

Jack: *I was feeling panicky. I mean I have a lot of skills. I've been in a lot of different kinds of situations, but I've never been in this kind. I didn't know what to do. As I said a minute ago, I have this fellow escalating, getting more frustrated, and I knew he wasn't going to be able to communicate. So I was getting a little panicky about how I was going to handle this situation. By the time I left, he had calmed down, so that part of it I'm okay with. I was able to take care of that. I was able to calm him down. Part of my struggle is that I'm holding on to this, and I'm not able to let go of it. And I have a history of being able to let go. I don't usually take things home. I kind of know intellectually that I can't be responsible for this kind of situation. This person was dying, had lost his ability to communicate, and I can't expect myself to be able to translate a language that neither he nor I knows.*

Marijane: *So what are you holding right now? What are the feelings in there right now?*

Jack: *Well, just sitting here talking about it kind of recreates some of those feelings.*

Marijane: *Which are…*

Jack: *Frustration is one of them, and I've said that about half a dozen times now, but I know there are more feelings. I think one of the other feelings is one of sadness. There's sadness there that there was a loss.*

Marijane: *A loss of…*

Jack: *Well, I'm not sure. I think my first reaction is to tag the loss on to what happened in that situation. But I kind of wonder whether the loss might be tied in somehow with something else, something about me.*

Marijane: *That could be a place we may want to focus.*

Supervision session ends.

Marijane: *One of the things I often find as a supervisor is that where my supervisee really needs me to go changes. First I really need to do some listening and use some listening skills, and there's some validation that's part of that and trying to get together with where the supervisee is. The dialog may start in one direction. At this point some supervisees are so well trained that they'll say, "Here's what I want," or they'll say, "I don't know what I want. I just know that this is not okay." So I figure it's real important that I don't choose the direction unless we have an ethical/legal problem or we only have five more minutes. I try to keep myself out of it because if I choose, it's coming out of me and my experience, and I really don't know what it's like for my supervisee. I truly don't. The more I don't know and the more I keep myself convinced that I don't know, the better supervisor I think I am. When I think I know what a supervisee needs, I'm going to get in there and start directing and controlling. I don't think that's as helpful as facilitating a supervisee's process.*

Jack: *I think you're right about giving more and more responsibility to the supervisee and not just taking it all on. You don't have to solve it all. You don't have to put all the pieces together. Put trust in the process because it tends to work itself out.*

SIT 1: *All of these things one does in counseling, so I'm kind of confused.*

Marijane: *So what you're picking up on is how your counseling skills are really helpful to you as a supervisor. What you're doing in supervision is going to be different. As a counselor, your focus is on the client. As a supervisor, your focus is on the supervisee.*

Jack: *We use our counseling skills whether we're teaching, counseling, or consulting, but the way we use them is a little bit different and goes back to the difference between counseling and supervision. Although we cannot be our supervisees' therapist, we can counsel them around issues related to their treatment of clients.*

SIT 2: *So toward the end part when you were kind of struggling, and you mention the word* loss, *would it have been okay to say, "So how are you going to grieve that?"*

Marijane: *That would be choosing, wouldn't it? Is that what he needed?*

Jack: *Maybe just open it up? Just open "loss" up. Just a simple reflection.*

SIT 3: *It almost presents a good opportunity to say, "Wow, you've put a lot of different things on the table here. There's this and this and this. Do you want to focus on one of those right now?"*

Jack: *Yes, that kind of intervention opens things up and gives the supervisee a chance to decide.*

Marijane: *And in a way, what is happening is that we're constantly refocusing because as Jack gets a little clearer about something, then he's ready, maybe, to focus a little differently. So as a supervisor, you're ready to shift to go where he needs to go, and he may not have known he needed to go there two minutes ago. And then it may change in two more minutes.*

SIT 4: *But at the same time, we're kind of chartered with the responsibility of keeping track of structure.*

Demonstration ends.

Beginning Supervision Checklist

You've been reading about many ideas for the shaping of clinical supervision and doing exercises to increase your learning of this process. The following is a chronological listing of preparation tasks for your first supervision session. You may want to add or eliminate some items, depending on your individual situation.

I've done this.	This is not needed.	Item
		Prepared a supervision disclosure statement
		Gave copy of disclosure statement to the supervisee
		Provided "Choosing a Supervisor" list to supervisee
		Gave supervisee the handout on preparing for supervision
		Secured a private space for sessions and for audio- or videotaping
		Read over the "Preparation for the Supervisor" segment of this section and formed my plan for the session
		Asked supervisee to fill out the "Intake" and bring it to our session
		Asked supervisee to come prepared to discuss cultural background

Focusing on the Supervisee

Even though you are ready to begin, you may find yourself struggling with these ideas. Most practitioners encounter some dissonance between their experiences as a supervisee and a supervisor and what we are advocating, particularly about focusing on the supervisee and the supervisee's dilemma. You have been trained as a counselor or therapist to focus on the client or client system, and this contributes to the dissonance. Now as a supervisor you are changing your focus from the client to the issues, dilemmas, and growth of the supervisee.

Practice Examples

The examples below can help you prepare for this new focus on the supervisee at the same time as you balance client welfare. You may choose to discuss the different responses in a small group.

Curiosity

Supervisee: *My client is always talking about how rich his family is and what prominence it has. Just the name is enough to scare me.*

Supervisor A: *What is the name?*

Supervisor B: *Let's talk a bit about the scariness. Intimidated?*

Comment: A asks for useless information. B focuses on an issue for the supervisee. We recognize that supervisors have to overcome the need to satisfy their curiosity when information is not important to facilitate supervisee growth.

No Problem

Supervisee: *Everything seems to be going fine. I don't have any issues that we really need to talk about today. I would have canceled but I was here anyway so I thought I'd drop in and tell you.*

Supervisor A: *OK. Well, if there isn't anything, I'm sure we can both use the time. Same time next week?*

Supervisor B: *As we go through your clients, you might take a bit of time and think of where you would like your learning to focus.*

Comment: Although the temptation may be to use the time in other ways, this may turn out to be the best session yet. We wonder what this is all about for the supervisee (and the supervisor if he or she chooses A).

Helping

Supervisee: *My client's mother wants to know of a good doctor for gallbladder trouble. I said I'd ask you.*

Supervisor A: *Dr. X operated on my friend. She liked him.*

Supervisor B:	*I don't have an answer for you, but it sounds like you are trying very hard to help. I wonder if that "helping" works both for and against you. Let's talk about that a bit.*
Comment:	It will be important to explore why this supervisee is working so hard to be perceived as a helper—even for gallbladder surgery! As supervisors, we need to be aware of and curious about behavior that seems out of context or unusual.

Dress Designer

Supervisee:	*My client Barbara is a dress designer. I'm really amazed at what she accomplishes. And her parents don't even seem to notice it. Her husband says they should understand how important the money she makes is to their grandson's education. She brought in some designs for me to see. They really blew my mind. She's so talented and....*
Supervisor A:	*Are those the designs? I've never seen such creations.*
Supervisor B:	*What is the issue or question that you would like us to focus on about your work with this client?*
Comment:	Some supervisees tend to give too much detail, and we are left floundering, wondering where we are going. At such times, supervisors need to interrupt and assist the supervisee in focusing.

Turmoil

Supervisee:	*You wouldn't believe what's been going on at my school since I came here last. The teachers are at each other all the time. The school board is railing on us. And the principal—well, he is no help at all. (More conversation about the principal.) There! I just needed to vent. I'm done.*
Supervisor A:	*Is he new to the school?*
Supervisor B:	*What are some ways you see this turmoil affecting your work with clients?*
Comment:	Focusing on the principal would just bring more venting. Focusing on how the situation affects the supervisee's work with clients is a productive focus.

I Quit

Supervisee:

I just came in today to let you know that I'll be dropping practicum. I know this is the seventh week, and I'll lose my money, but I've found out I need to leave the program. I thought I could be a good counselor, but I just can't. You are teaching us that we aren't supposed to tell the clients what to do, but that is all I know how to do. I really don't fit here. Everyone else is doing so well. I just feel really, really stupid.

Supervisor A:

Hey! Don't cry. You're doing great. You're just having a bad day. Look, let's go get a cup of coffee and dry those tears. You really are just fine.

Supervisor B:

I appreciate your coming in and sharing this. It took a lot of courage. It sounds like there is more than one issue. I hear you saying you feel inadequate with clients, not as competent as your classmates, and pretty alone in this whole process. Which one brings the most concern for you?

Comment:

Supervisor A uses praise and invalidates the supervisee's concerns. Supervisor B shows that the concerns have been heard, demonstrates respect by acceptance of the supervisee's issues, and allows the supervisee to choose focus. Thus Supervisor B gives the supervisee an opportunity to understand the complexity of the issues or dilemmas being experienced.

Flattery

Supervisee:

You are just wonderful. I told my mother how lucky I was to have such a great supervisor. When you demonstrate an intervention, it blows my mind. I want to be just like you. I just want you to know that.

Supervisor A:

What was it I said that you liked?

Supervisor B:

What was an intervention that you did this last week with your clients that you felt worked especially well?

Comment:

Flattery can feel good to us, and we may even seek more as Supervisor A does, but it doesn't help with our work. Supervisor B turns the focus over to a successful intervention of the supervisee's.

It is important for supervisees to notice what they do that works well so that they can do more of it.

Referral

Supervisee: *I received a referral from a colleague. This client is an American who lives in Norway and wants to do counseling over the telephone and/or the Internet. I have given this a lot of thought and have decided not to accept the referral.*

Supervisor A: *Sounds like you have made a decision. Are you ready to move on?*

Supervisor B: *You have told me that you have made a decision on this referral, and yet you chose to bring it up in supervision. Would you like to discuss this further?*

Comment: Supervisor A ignores the fact that the supervisee chose to bring this issue to supervision, even though it was stated that a decision had been made. However, Supervisor B acknowledges that the supervisee thought this decision was important enough to bring to supervision and offers the supervisee a chance to explore it further. We find when a supervisee brings anything to supervision, there usually is a reason that is worth exploring.

Departing

Supervisee: *I have a client in her sixties who is considering leaving her husband of 40 years. He has been accused of molesting children, and, as a consequence, my client has limited access to her grandchildren. I feel myself encouraging her to leave him. I don't know whether I am helping her, or am I just responding to my own feelings?*

Supervisor A: *Talk about both sides.*

Supervisor B: *My sense is that you are on the right track. This guy sounds like a loser, and she deserves to see her grandchildren.*

Comment: While Supervisor B's intervention may be accurate, it ignores the question raised by the supervisee. This could be a serious oversight, since there could be some countertransference that may not be conscious or visible. Supervisor A's intervention is designed to open up the possibility of some countertransference and, at the very least, to provide the opportunity for the supervisee to answer the question of why this dilemma was important enough to bring to supervision.

Reluctant

Supervisee: *I know you said to ask our clients about suicide as a part of our intake, but I'm concerned about how they may react. Won't they be embarrassed? If I ask them, could I give them the idea, and might they go and do it? Won't this adversely affect our relationship?*

Supervisor A: *You seem to be concerned about bringing up suicide with your clients. I wonder what you are afraid of.*

Supervisor B: *These are typical concerns. I would like to address each one in order to lower your anxiety.*

Comment: Supervisor B's intervention certainly addresses the supervisee's questions directly. We believe such an intervention would be helpful, but our preference would be Supervisor A's intervention. While the question and concerns have some relevance, they are all focused on the client. We prefer to begin by focusing on the supervisee, and once the fear/anxiety has been processed, we might speak briefly about the myths surrounding assessing suicide ideation with clients.

No Plan

Supervisee: *I completed an intake on a 17-year-old girl. During the assessment, she admitted she often thinks about killing herself. Although she said she didn't have a plan, she indicated that she was evaluated for suicide and briefly hospitalized. Her parents accompanied her to the assessment and confirmed the prior hospitalization. What do you think? Do you think I can handle this case?*

Supervisor A: *Sounds like you completed a thorough assessment and would like to take on this young woman as your client.*

Supervisor B: *How about you? What are your thoughts about assuming the responsibility as her therapist?*

Comment: Supervisor A's intervention is reasonable and may work. We believe that its weakness is the fact that it does not directly address the supervisee's implied concern. Supervisor B's intervention gently shifts the focus back to the supervisee and asks the supervisee to explore the concerns that motivated him or her to bring up the case in supervision.

Discouraged

Supervisee:	*I am seeing a young man who is very different from my other clients in that he is bright, articulate, and interesting. I enjoy working with him and look forward to my sessions. He is a recovering alcoholic, on methadone, depressed, with no friends or family support, and his wife just filed for divorce. He was a physician's assistant but lost his license because of misappropriation of drugs.*
Supervisor A:	*You are using language like "bright," "articulate, "interesting," and "enjoy" when talking about this client. What do you think this means in terms of your relationship?*
Supervisor B:	*First, I would like us to look at your client's potential for committing suicide. Have you conducted a harm assessment?*
Comment:	This situation presents two possible directions for the supervisor. The initial information is related to supervisee language that may indicate attraction. This may or may not be the case and is important to explore at some point. The priority that both the counselor and the supervisor have in this situation is an obligation to address the safety of this client. Since the client seems to be struggling in most areas of his life, he is a prime candidate for committing suicide. Both the supervisee and supervisor need to address this issue first.

Sleepless

Supervisee:	*My client is a 40-year-old male who has been in and out of the hospital's psychiatric unit since his son committed suicide in front of him. My client is an alcoholic, depressed, suicidal, and has given up hope. He is not changing, and I don't know what to do to help. The worst part of this case is that I am taking it home with me, and it is interfering with my sleep.*
Supervisor A:	*Sounds like you are feeling hopeless and discouraged yourself.*
Supervisor B:	*Describe what you have been doing with him.*
Comment:	This is another case where both interventions could work. Supervisor A chose to focus on the supervisee's feelings, which could help the supervisee to look at the countertransference and/or at least acknowledge the situation and how it feels when a client has very few or no options. Supervisor B's intervention moves the

supervisee in a different direction, in that it forces the supervisee to look at both himself and his client from a different angle. This may provide the opportunity for some supervisee movement by assisting in the creation of a plan.

Abandoned

Supervisee:	*I recently had a client whom I had seen several times and who had disclosed some very personal information. He also told me he planned to leave the state for another job. Though I had anticipated he would be leaving, I felt abandoned when he left without coming into the office or even calling me to say goodbye.*
Supervisor A:	*You say you felt abandoned by the client. What are the feelings you are expressing?*
Supervisor B:	*Sounds like you were heavily invested in this client.*
Comment:	This is a difficult choice. We feel that Supervisor A's intervention is the more appropriate, because it encompasses both data gathering and exploration. We believe that it is important to be patient and to allow the process to unfold, as it usually provides more avenues to explore, and these are often more opportunities for learning. Supervisor B's intervention is more direct and focused, and though it may be both accurate and helpful, it would cut off other avenues of exploration.

All the practice examples demonstrate the principal of keeping the focus on the supervisee—not the client, not the situation, not the supervisor. That does not mean that we never need to know something about the client, the situation, or the supervisory relationship. It simply means that most of the time we keep the focus on the supervisee while we attend to the development of the supervisee, client welfare, and the supervision process.

Creative Responses to Facilitate Supervision

Throughout this section of the book we have been focusing on what the supervisor will be doing during the supervision session. Most of the interventions that have been demonstrated have had a cognitive focus. The interactive exercises have a similar emphasis. We believe that many supervisors enhance the learning potential of supervisees by the use of unique and creative responses. In order to assist you in developing your creativity, we invite you to participate in the right brain focus of artwork and sandplay in individual and group formats.

Artwork

Creative interventions in supervision can provide an effective way of delivering three functions of supervision: (1) a formative function, (2) a supportive or restorative function, and (3) a normative or managerial function (Wilkins, 1995). The formative function is concerned with reflection on and exploration of the work of supervisees with their clients. As an example of this function, we might grab a pad of paper and draw a representation of what we hear the supervisee saying. "So it sounds like you are over here, and the client has you blocked off from movement, sort of like this drawing." The reflection can provide a visual representation of the dilemma or issue. The supportive or restorative function can alleviate the emotional stress of working as a therapist. One example of artwork with this function would be to ask the supervisee to describe what a balanced career would be like at this juncture using the art medium. The normative or managerial function of delivering quality services to clients might be represented when a supervisor asked a supervisee to use art media to describe the tension between the administrative and clinical portions of his job. Artwork can be a useful addition to a supervisor's creative repertoire both for individual and group expression during supervision.

Directions to the supervisee: Use the media to represent your question, concern, problem, or dilemma.

An Example

At midterm we asked practicum students to use media to represent where they saw themselves in relation to becoming a professional in the field. The students were allotted 15 minutes for the activities, and each had his or her own set of all four listed mediums. The directive of "no talking" was the only rule in order to allow students silence for individual reflection.

The results were compared to pictures at the end of practicum, seven weeks later. As students described their drawings, we found that we, the professors, learned far more than if we had asked a question, but the more important result was the student insight that was gained. Students reported that the drawings had elements of connection and truth that were previously unrecognized. We were sold. This was a valuable use of group supervision time for the practicum students.

Materials:
- Colored pencils
- Colored markers (preferably both fat and thin sizes)
- Craypas or a similar colored chalk-like medium
- Crayons
- Large paper, preferably 12" x 18" as a minimum

We invite you to try this exercise. Draw a representation of where you see yourself as a supervisor at this moment in time. This also can be used as a group exercise.

- Describe the experience of creating your drawing.
- What new awareness resulted from this exercise?
- When might you use such an exercise with your supervisees?

Following are suggestions related to the use of artwork in supervision.

This activity may be helpful in the following areas:

- Practicum classes
- Internship classes
- Individual supervisees in their probationary periods

Some situations in which artwork may be facilitative:

- To assist an individual or group at an impasse
- To describe the relationship between the supervisee and the work environment

Peer Group Supervision: A New Format

Before beginning this section, take time to reflect on your group supervision and peer group supervision experiences. Since your experiences may differ from those in the literature, note the advantages and disadvantages of any group supervision experiences you have had. This would be a helpful topic to reflect on and discuss in a group.

Advantages and disadvantages for me

Peer supervision groups provide both clear advantages and disadvantages for the development of counseling knowledge and skills. On one hand, these groups offer a solution that can meet proximity and availability requirements with little or no cost. Peer group members can provide new ideas for working with difficult or confusing cases, a forum for discussion of ethical and legal questions, and an atmosphere that is conducive to professional growth. On the other hand, there are drawbacks to this format. Inconsistent attendance and leadership, casual chitchat, lack of structure, overly supportive feedback, and advice giving are all possibly problematic for counselor development. Borders (1991) proposed a systematic approach that maximizes the strengths and minimizes the weaknesses of peer group supervision. The structured peer group format has the following advantages:

- Ensures all members are involved
- Emphasizes focused and objective feedback
- Emphasizes cognitive counseling skills
- Can be used with groups of experienced and inexperienced counselors
- Provides a framework for supervisors
- Teaches an approach for self-monitoring

Borders's (1991) format is frequently used with groups of 3 to 6 counselors and one facilitator or supervisor. When the group is time-limited and includes up to 12 individuals, prioritizing issues that group members bring is an important first step. In turn, counselors become the supervisee while the rest of the group members become peer supervisors. The abbreviated procedure is as follows:

1. One counselor (supervisee) describes an issue or question on which the counselor wishes feedback.

2. A designated leader is the timekeeper and assigns roles, perspectives, or tasks for the peers to assume when giving feedback. Frequently assigned roles are the spouse, parent, friend, supervisor, client or counselor, a metaphor, or a particular theoretical orientation.

3. The supervisee describes the issue in more detail and repeats the question or issue for feedback. An audiotape or videotape segment may be used to augment the description.

4. Peers give feedback from their assigned perspectives.

4. The supervisee summarizes the feedback from peers and discusses its meaning.

6. The designated leader may or may not choose to facilitate a discussion.

The auditory feedback received by the supervisee is nonevaluative, is specific to the question or issue of the supervisee, and presents new perspectives. The supervisee is free to interpret the feedback. When we teach these steps we like to emphasize that this is theatre. Group members play out their roles as they would in theatre, creating background where there is none. The accuracy and fullness of the background information is not relevant, since the focus is providing diverse perspectives from which the supervisee can choose to make relevant decisions to resolve the question or dilemma. The goal is to provide a variety of data that one can draw on at any time. It is as though the role-players are making deposits to the supervisee's bank account from which the supervisee may draw. It is the supervisee's job to make meaning out of the information received from the role-play.

We use this format for peer groups when we are teaching supervision as well as in practicum and internship. Frequently assigned roles when teaching supervision are lawyer, ethics review board member, supervisor in the teaching mode, supervisor in the counseling mode, supervisor in the consultation mode, as well as the roles in the above list of steps for counselors. Since learning is often enhanced when other modalities of teaching are utilized, we have added the role of the sandtray to Borders's original list of roles.

There are five principal reasons for utilizing the sandtray:

1. Sand is a creative medium that fosters right brain activity.

2. Children and adults are able to express previously unrecognized thoughts and feelings in the sand.

3. Supervisees are presented with a visual representation of the issue or question. We know that many individuals are more dependent on visual cues than on auditory cues.

4. Supervisees in workshops, classes, or private practice consistently report that the sandtray image is the most powerful of all the feedback responses.

5. Supervisees appear to lower defenses and accept the visual feedback.

We consistently find that the visual representation from the sandtray was the most valuable feedback for the supervisee. A few comments are listed here.

- *Suddenly I saw my issue in a whole new way.*

- *The sandbox was the most valuable for me.*

- *When I was assigned the role of the sandbox I didn't know what I would do. But my fingers kept picking, choosing, and placing objects. I was so surprised by the result, and it blew my peer away.*

- *I didn't want to stop. It was almost as though I was alone in the room, even though people were talking. I love this!*

An example of a sandtray response. This picture was a peer group member's illustration of what was going on between the supervisee (counselor) and her client. In the sandtray the supervisee has turned her back on the reality of sharks and the octopus that are ready to attack her client's child. In addition, there is a separation (the marbles) between the client and her child and the counselor.

When the supervisee viewed the sandtray, she was struck by the fact that the counselor (the supervisee in this moment) was turning her back on the client. She immediately connected to this with the statement that she was trying so hard to keep a focus on the client that she was in reality ignoring her, since the client was concerned with the dangers for the child. This insight enabled the supervisee to develop a plan that included both client focus and the client's concern. In effect she joined with the client while keeping this client focus.

Materials to gather for sandtray. Much has been written about the therapeutic medium of sandtray and the necessary equipment. For the tray, we have used such plastic storage materials as clear plastic boxes. At one site we have figures and objects in small plastic boxes surrounding the sand. At another site we utilize a very large basket and many small plastic containers within, filled with useful objects and figures. This combination works well and is portable, and such materials can be gathered quickly and easily. Some of our favorite materials are listed below.

Suggestions for Sandtray Items
People of various sizes and skin colors
Animals, especially families of animals with differing sizes, both for land and water
Materials for boundaries such as fences, sticks, rocks
Specialty items, such as a wine glass or beer bottle, magic wand, sword
Crystal ball (especially helpful in supervision)
Vehicles such as army tanks, fire trucks, ambulances, police cars
Specialty figures such as a fairy godmother, villain, police officer, medical person
Materials from nature such as dried plants, shells, rocks
Marbles
Other

Group Exercise

Since we learn best by experiencing that which we are learning, we invite your class or group to try out this model of peer group supervision. After completing supervision of one individual, you may find it helpful to stop and discuss the activity and refine the process. Proceed, giving other group members a chance to present a case or dilemma. Questions for group discussion following the activity are listed below:

1. What was it like to experience peer group supervision with this model?

2. What did you learn about yourself?

3. Compare the experience of receiving auditory-only feedback to the experience of receiving auditory and visual feedback from the medium of the sand.

4. What are some other ways you bring auditory and visual experience together when supervising?

Sandtray Work with Individuals

The use of sandtray work in supervision is a relatively new idea. We know that sand can be a creative medium for expression for all the reasons listed previously concerning the peer group supervison intervention. However, knowing something cognitively and believing it can be two different things. A personal illustration that convinced one author of the efficacy of this intervention technique follows:

Laura, a counselor of 15 years, was training as a supervisor. She always came to her supervision sessions well prepared with a listing of agenda items to tackle. On this day she was describing an apparent supervisee reluctance to explore the depths of an issue. I asked Laura what the relationship was like between her and her supervisee. This question left her absolutely stuck. She was unable to answer at all.

I tried to assist her in exploring this issue and found us equally stuck. It was then that my eye caught a glimpse of the sandtray in the corner. (We were in a room frequently used for counseling children through play.) I brought the sandtray over to Laura along with some figures and asked her to show me in the sand what the relationship looked like. She looked puzzled at first and then set to work designing a sandtray that depicted a figure, identified as herself, with her back to another figure, identified as the supervisee with whom she was working. She had constructed a wall between the two figures, representing some of her fears.

After she completed the sandtray and explanation, I asked her what she would like to change in the depiction in the sand and how she thought it might proceed. She thought and then moved the figures side by side by blasting a pathway through her fears. "There! I've done it!" she exclaimed. "I didn't even know those were there (the fears), but I know they will not be as influential in our next session." At that moment I became a believer in the use of the sandtray as an intervention in supervision. That medium had facilitated the supervisee's opening up of previously inaccessible material that my questions had not exposed.

We, the authors of this text, both have sandtrays in rooms we use for supervision. We do not have a huge selection of materials to use in the sand, but find that a selection such as mentioned in the previous section on peer group supervision suffices. Topics that lend themselves to sandtray exploration in supervision are listed below, but allow your creativity to add others.

1. What would the relationship between you and the client look like in the sand?
2. What happened in that session? Describe the session in the sand.
3. How do you think the client would depict the relationship?
4. How would you depict the relationship between you and me?
5. If you wished for change in that sandtray depiction, what might you do?

An Example

Supervisee: *I'm really struggling in my relationship with my client, Jane. It seems like she doesn't want to even be there. Actually it's more like she wishes I weren't there and someone else was. She seems to just prattle on and not even recognize where I am trying to assist her. I'm really stumped as to how to proceed.*

Supervisor: *Talk some more about the relationship. What is it like for you to be there in the space with her?*

Supervisee (long pause): *Boy, that's a tough one. I like her, but I guess she's not the kind of person I would choose for a friend.*

Supervisor: *So there you are, sitting with this person you wouldn't choose for a friend. Help me understand what it feels like to sit there with her.*

Supervisee (longer pause): *This is really tough. There's not really any feeling I can come up with.*

Supervisor: *Would you be willing to try an experiment? I wonder if you could try to illustrate what it's like when you are together in your session with the sandtray over there. There are some things you could use in the basket.*

Supervisee: *I have been wondering when you would let me use that! Hummm. (Sets to work placing figures in the sandtray, moving them around, adding fences, changing figures, stopping after a bit, pointing to the sandtray he has completed.) That's what it's like! I'm over here, this little boy, and I keep trying to walk toward her but can't get close. And she's this larger woman character. There's a stone wall between us. So she talks, but I can't get over to where she is. Just looking at it makes me realize how awful I feel in there.*

Supervisor: *What would you like the relationship to look like?*

Supervisee: *I'd like to be much closer, be equal in height, sort of equals working on this problem, like this (showing in the sand by replacing the boy figure with a man figure of equal height to the woman figure).*

Supervisor: *Now that you know what you want and know where you currently are, can you think of anything you could do to assist with getting closer to the relationship you wish to have?*

Supervisee: *Well, for one thing, I don't need to be a boy. I think I am intimidated by her rapid delivery. It's like I'm not important, I guess. I don't think I have realized that I was internalizing that feeling. I suspect that her delivery is because she is anxious a bit, or maybe it's a pattern she is always using.*

Supervisor (smiling): *So it sounds like you are planning to grow up the next time you meet. Do you have any ideas what might help with that change in perception?*

Supervisee: *I suspect I've already begun to do it. Just seeing myself in the sandtray as a little boy makes me realize that I was bringing about this distant relationship, not her. I think it will be very different next time. You know, in the past I've been dreading our appointments, and now I can't wait to see her!*

Group Exercise: Read the example of a sandtray dialog. Discuss the utility of such an intervention for you as a supervisor. Your group may wish to use a sandtray in the discussion, asking one person to represent an individual's dialog content in the sandtray.

Typical Problems in Supervision

Supervisee behavior is unique during each supervision session. At the same time, we have found that there are often consistent behaviors that evolve and develop from session to session, some of which inhibit supervision. This consistency provides the supervisor the opportunity to identify, address, and resolve typical problems. Following is a series of typical supervisee growth-inhibiting behaviors that we have experienced in our practices. We provide brief definitions of these behaviors, followed by suggestions of ways supervisors can assist supervisees in reducing or eliminating them. We encourage you to reflect on what we have written and to develop your own responses or interventions given the individuality of your supervisees and their problems.

What to Do When There Is Conflict in the Supervisory Relationship

Conflict in the supervisory relationship is both unavoidable and desirable; in fact, it may even be supervision's most important process (Bernard & Goodyear, 2004). It appears unavoidable since there is an evaluation component to the hierarchical relationship, and two people will not always agree. The desirability may be that in recognizing the conflict, naming it, allowing it, not judging it, and processing it we are modeling a relationship dynamic that can only strengthen our collaboration. However, conflict is a dynamic that elicits discomfort in many therapists and supervisors.

In the examples that follow, supervisees express concerns that may lead to conflict.

Supervisee: *I know you said we need to work from goals, but that is not how I usually do it.*

Supervisee: *I didn't do the mental status part of the intake. She was doing fine. I didn't think there was any reason to ask her those questions. Besides, it might scare her away.*

Supervisee: *I know we talked about getting a release of information before I talked to the lawyer, but it worked out a little differently. The lawyer came by before the mother, but she said she was going to sign the release when I talked with her over the telephone. The bad part is that she still hasn't come in. I didn't say too much to him though.*

In all these situations, the supervisee may or may not be aware that there is conflict. Resolution may occur through self-reflection by the supervisee. Resolution also may come when a supervisor decides to change behaviors in the supervisory session, and this leads to a different perception by the supervisee. However, it is our experience that conflict will often need to be dealt with explicitly. It is the supervisor's role to acknowledge it.

Supervisor: *It sounds like we have a conflict here. Let's talk about that.*

Supervisor: *So it sounds like you weren't feeling okay about my suggestions last week.*

Sometimes conflict is expressed in a more passive manner. Supervisees may always be late, may cancel appointments, may not be doing required paperwork, or may be giving a perfunctory response to the supervisor. Although these symptoms do not necessarily mean conflict, they are important to investigate by using immediacy. Opening up a discussion should be a helpful intervention.

Supervisor: *I wonder whether we could talk about what's going on here in supervision between us. I sense we are experiencing a bit of turbulence. What has your experience been?*

Although working through conflict is always done thoughtfully with respect for the other person's privacy, it can result in a strengthened relationship between the supervisee and supervisor. Bernard and Goodyear (1998) state that this weakening and repair of working alliance between supervisor and supervisee may be supervision's most important process. We agree, but we are always rewarded with a more connected relationship. That does not mean that disputes always are resolved immediately. They are not. The beginning discussion may lead to change on the part of either or both supervisor and supervisee after reflection subsequent to supervision. What is our advice if you are experiencing conflict in the supervisory relationship? Open it up, and remember that supervisors deserve supervision also.

What to Do When Your Supervisee Is Overly Dependent

There is much written in the literature concerning the hierarchical nature of the relationship between the supervisee and the supervisor. The supervisor's responsibility to evaluate is influential in creating this dynamic, as is the fact that most supervisors are older and have more years of experience than their supervisees. These relationship characteristics may create a variety of transactional dynamics, including supervisee dependency on the supervisor. Given the above characteristics, some dependency is normal and expected. Yet when a supervisee begins to give up responsibility and expects the supervisor to assume that responsibility, the effectiveness of the supervision is in jeopardy. Monitoring dependency in the supervisory relationship requires diligence on the part of the supervisor. We have listed below a number of supervisee and supervisor behaviors to watch for as indicators of possible dependency between the supervisee and supervisor as well as suggestions on how to respond should any of these situations arise.

1. Repetitive supervisee questions/statements such as:
   a. What do I do now?
   b. How do you do this?
   c. I don't know how to do this.
   d. I'm confused/lost.

   Suggestion: Although the temptation is to answer the question directly, turn the question or the statement back to the supervisee. In doing so, you will be encouraging the supervisee to take on the responsibility he or she is trying to give up.

2. The supervisee consistently defers to the supervisor.
   a. What do you think?
   b. I can't think of anything to do.

   Suggestion: Even though it may feel good to be held in deference, be persistent in deferring back to the supervisee. If this is not successful, discuss your observations with the supervisee and explore the need to defer.

3. Supervisees who consistently discount their own competence.
   a. I don't do this very well.
   b. You do this so much better than I do.

   Suggestion: This behavior is usually designed to elicit a positive response from the supervisor. Often not responding to the supervisee will be helpful, or if this behavior persists, you may have to discuss the dynamic directly with him or her.

4. Supervisees seeing their supervisor as Mom or Dad.

   Suggestion: This could be a classic countertransference situation. It is important to point this out to the supervisee and process it.

5. Supervisee resistance to making decisions without first contacting the supervisor and/or supervisees who make frequent contact with their supervisors.

   Suggestion: Encourage your supervisees to make more decisions on their own. Discuss with supervisees their need to be in frequent contact with you.

6. Supervisor feelings of
   a. "I have all the responsibility."
   b. "I am feeling overwhelmed!"
   c. "This supervisee is high maintenance."

   Suggestion: Conduct your own self-reflection on your level of responsibility. Ask yourself whether you are assuming responsibility that rightfully belongs to your supervisee. Seek supervision or consultation from a respected colleague. Establish new boundaries as necessary.

We believe that supervisors need to be keenly aware of signs and circumstances of supervisee dependence and reliance on the supervisor as a source of power and self-learning. The act of supervision provides the opportunity for the growth of skills and knowledge through the supervisee's own resources. This progress is an act of empowerment that supervisors must allow for in their approach to assisting trainees in maximizing their own resources.

What to Do When Your Supervisee Is Not Taking Risks in Learning

Not taking risks in learning is a situation that often occurs with students or recent graduates. More experienced practitioners usually have discovered that if they want to grow in professional knowledge and skill, they have to take risks. To risk is to change, and few of us ever begin that process willingly. Added to that is the student's dilemma of, "If I disclose all of my weaknesses, my professor will think I am an incompetent counselor and give me a low grade." There are other important variables that influence the level of risk-taking, such as confidence, self-esteem, and courage. The challenge for us as supervisors is to assist our supervisees in summoning the courage to accept the risk to enhance learning.

We invite you to consider the following suggestions:

1. Our first suggestion is preventative in nature. The university professor has a formidable challenge in managing the dual relationship of supervisor and evaluator. We feel the professor's best way of managing this situation is through talking about it in an open, honest manner early and throughout the relationship. The key is to involve supervisees in an ongoing dialogue.

2. Another useful technique is to discuss the lack of risk-taking with supervisees, and to encourage them to make this a goal in their supervision plan. More important is to maintain ongoing dialogue with supervisees as a way of assisting them in overcoming their fears.

3. A technique we have found useful and that goes hand in hand with 1 and 2 is encouragement. Encouragement, as opposed to praise, focuses on developing an internal reward system and emphasizes how supervisees are thinking and feeling about a situation. For example, a supervisor might say to a supervisee, "You seem to feel good about how that series of interventions went with your client." This allows supervisees to focus on themselves and their internal reward systems and not to rely on their supervisors.

4. A similar but different technique is affirmation. This is not praise but has praise-like qualities, since it does come from an external source. Affirmation is most effective when it is focused on the supervisee's behavior rather than on the supervisee as a person. The goal of this intervention is to assist supervisees in developing the confidence and courage to take the risk of allowing the supervisor to see them when they are vulnerable. An example would be a supervisor saying, "Your intervention challenged your client to stop and think about the consequences of her actions."

Supervisees who are not taking risks to learn can be challenging for supervisors, as this behavior jeopardizes the major goal of supervision, the growth and development of the supervisee. This is a situation we as supervisors cannot ignore. Our actions need to be thoughtful and creative. We need to help supervisees find a way around their fear. Our experience as supervisors is that supervisees respond more quickly when we are honest with them about our observations and have the courage to bring them to their attention. The result is collaboration, and, when coupled with encouragement and affirmation, supervisee risk taking is likely to follow.

What to Do When Your Supervisee Feels Anxious

Supervisee anxiety is pervasive, especially for student supervisees in practicum and internship. After all, these students are being observed and evaluated in ways they likely have never experienced before. They may be required to tape all their sessions, transcribe parts of sessions, and complete intakes, case notes, and case summaries. They have been thrust into a new setting that is foreign to most people, where acclimating oneself is a major task.

In addition to all the external factors, there are two internal situations that often are anxiety producing for students. The first is that they have spent most of their academic careers in knowledge-based courses, and now they must prove they can actually do what they came to graduate school to learn to do. The second internal factor is that many students harbor the irrational belief that when they counsel, they will be omnipotent and make a difference in every client's life. Given all these internal and external considerations, is it any wonder that student supervisees feel anxious? Thus the challenge for us as supervisors is to recognize and assist our supervisees in reducing their anxiety.

We invite you to consider the following suggestions:

1. One of the best ways to reduce supervisees' anxiety is to dialogue with them and encourage them to talk about their fears. Just allowing supervisees to talk about what they are experiencing can have a dramatic effect in reducing anxiety. This is best done early in the relationship. For example, "You seem anxious about all the work in practicum. I wonder whether you would talk about that a bit?"

2. Supervisor support can be a way of reducing supervisee anxiety. Showing understanding about supervisees' challenging situations and communicating encouragement and affirmation are examples of supervisor support.

3. Working with supervisees in a more collaborative way often reduces supervisee anxiety. Using the role of consultation whenever appropriate is an example of how collaboration may be accomplished.

4. Goal setting with supervisees can be helpful, because it reduces the magnitude of what they are doing and makes tasks seem less open-ended and formidable.

5. Clearly stating role expectations is another way of placing some limits on what often seems like a limitless environment.

6. Providing supervisees with clear and relevant feedback also can have the effect of reducing anxiety.

7. Supervisors' self-disclosure about feelings of anxiety during their training can have the effect of normalizing anxiety and providing a stimulus for supervisees to see their anxiety in a different light.

8. Humor can assist supervisees in alleviating anxiety. A timely anecdote or article about the foibles of practicum/internship can help supervisees see humor in what otherwise may seem intimidating.

Anxiety is a powerful emotion in the learning process. We know we want our supervisees to feel some anxiety; however, too much can have serious negative consequences. Our task is to use our skills to help supervisees maintain a comfortable level of anxiety that will maximize their learning.

What to Do When Your Supervisee Is Not Prepared for Supervision

Although we do not like to think about our supervisees not being prepared, this occurs frequently and obligates us to take some action. Our initial reaction is often forbearance and, when the behavior continues, may turn into annoyance or frustration. These emotions often are a result of our expectations and/or supervisees' inability to communicate with us concerning their lack of preparation. A gentle exploration of the circumstances influencing the lack of preparation can be helpful in figuring out viable ways to work with our supervisees. We invite you to consider the following approaches:

1. Find out if your supervisee knows and understands what you mean by "being prepared." We have discovered that students and new counselors, even after some instruction, struggle to know how to prepare adequately or even what being prepared for supervision means. This lack of understanding may be complicated by other, less obvious factors that may need to be considered.

2. One of the primary reasons for the lack of preparation is the anxiety related to feeling unsafe. Our experience is that when supervisees are feeling unsafe, they will try to hide as much of their work and themselves as possible, and this comes across in supervision as not being prepared. Working directly with supervisees about feeling unsafe usually is helpful. It assists them in releasing enough of their anxiety in order to focus more on themselves and their development. Your perceptions of your supervisees' preparation will likely shift when they become more comfortable in taking risks.

3. There may be some personal issues that are interfering with the supervisees' preparation. This deserves careful and thorough review, as many inexperienced supervisees will not readily volunteer personal information. Even though

supervisees may need to work on these issues with an outside therapist, assisting them in being prepared for supervision is a priority.

4. Lack of preparation may be a result of discouragement, disorganization, or lack of commitment. We believe it is important for supervisors to explore with supervisees their individual situations and how these may be interfering with their preparation for supervision. Avoiding this discussion can be detrimental to supervisee development.

The theme for these four approaches is thoughtful exploration. If the lack of preparation is allowed to continue, supervisees' development may be truncated, and their future as mental health providers may be jeopardized. Lack of preparation is a situation in which the supervisor needs to take an active role with some immediacy. At the same time, careful analysis of the whole picture is in order, as the explanation of the behavior is seldom straightforward. A full understanding of all the factors provides the supervisor the best opportunity to influence supervisees.

What to Do When Your Supervisee Says, "Let's Go Grab a Cup of Coffee"

A unique dual relationship often is apparent for doctoral students supervising master's level peers. Prior to or during the supervision semester or year, supervisor and supervisee may be in classes and social gatherings as peers. In such situations it is easy to see how a supervisee may ask, "How about getting together for a cup of coffee and working on those research examples from class?"

One of us frequently refers to the "slippery slope" of dual relationships. Once on the slope, the slide to the bottom may be gradual and insidious. The cup of coffee and research examples may slide to an invitation to a movie and conversations that may leave the supervisory relationship cloudy at best. Client care as well as evaluation and gatekeeper functions of the supervisory role may be compromised. Although the literature on monitoring the dual relationship in supervision is not as clearly delineated as it is for the counseling relationship, the vision of a slippery slope is crucial to decision making around such situations. Your answer to such invitations will depend on your management of the dual relationship. Examples of possible responses follow:

1. *That's a tough one. On one hand, I'd love the chance to work with you on those research questions. On the other hand, I feel that our supervision relationship could be affected. So thanks, but I'll just have to work my way through those alone.*

2. *I really appreciate the offer, but I have an appointment then.*

3. *Sure. Maybe we could go out to dinner and that new movie afterwards.*

4. *Thanks. I really appreciate the offer. I think it would be best if we didn't meet.*

5. *Could we spend some time discussing the boundaries of our supervision relationship first so that we are both clear?*

It is our opinion that the third response should not be voiced. It does not reflect any consideration of the supervisory relationship. Although the second reply may be taking the easy road by not addressing the issue, perhaps the truth would be better for the relationship. Responses 1, 4, and 5 establish a boundary in a respectful manner toward the supervisee. Which will you choose? Be clear about your reasons. When supervising, note such decisions in your records.

A similar dual relationship can exist in agencies. Supervisors may be co-workers sharing in intra-agency functions and social and collegial relationships. We see the application of the same principles as crucial. It is the supervisor's responsibility to manage the boundaries and guidelines in such a way as to ensure clarity between both parties and both roles.

What to Do When Your Supervisee Fails to Follow Policies or Supervisor Recommendations

In most universities and agencies, there are definite responsibilities for supervisees. Two examples are: (1) clinical notes must be written on the day of the appointment and placed in the client's file, and (2) the supervisor is to be notified immediately in cases of suspected abuse or suicidal thoughts or behaviors. These examples of rules or behavior codes are typically nonnegotiable. Counseling students in many practicum and internship courses are faced with many such rules. How should supervisors respond when supervisees fail to carry out these or other directives?

Although it is important to listen to the supervisee, it also is necessary to restate the directive and ask how the supervisee will meet the requirement. In the first example below, the supervisee has not filed case notes in clients' records for the preceding sessions. This is an agency requirement as well as an ethical obligation.

Supervisee: *I just haven't been able to get to my notes. My baby has been ill, and I've rushed home after seeing clients in order to tend to her. I know I'm supposed to do the notes before leaving, but it just hasn't been possible. I should be better this coming week as the baby's fever broke last night, and I have just completed the notes for last week.*

Supervisor: *That sounds like a tough situation for you, balancing home and the agency. Since the rule has to be followed, how might you handle this another time?*

In a second example, a similar situation exists. The supervisee fails to implement supervisor suggestions.

Supervisor: *Last week we discussed and role-played how to ask the client about goals. How did that go?*

Supervisee: *Oh, I didn't do it. Truthfully, it feels kind of rude to force clients that way. I really prefer to just listen to them. I know she wanted that too so I went along with her.*

Supervisor: *I'm a bit troubled by this, This is the second time you haven't followed what we discussed. What's stopping you from doing this?*

This is one of those areas that most supervisors find uncomfortable. In the first example, the supervisor's over-identification with the supervisee and the supervisee's issues could lead the supervisor astray. Regardless of personal circumstances, the supervisee's behavior must change. She must follow agency guidelines even when personal problems interfere. The second situation is similar. The supervisor needs to reassert the original position of requiring the supervisee to address goals with the client. Supervisor persistence is important in assisting the supervisee in reflecting on and adhering to obligations.

What to Do When Your Supervisee Asks Questions

In general, we seek answers from individuals with more years of experience and greater expertise. These two conditions also lead to increased power in most sectors of society. The supervisory relationship by definition is not equal in both years of experience and power, the latter due to the evaluation and gatekeeper functions. Questions are voiced to the supervisor throughout the supervisory sessions for these reasons.

> *I've never worked with a person with such severe depression. I'm following Beck's recommendations, but I'm concerned that my inexperience results in inadequate treatment. Who are other authorities who have written about working with this population?*

> *The client just keeps telling stories about how her husband is wrong, and my attempts to refocus the session on her are unsuccessful. I'm wondering what I can do to get her looking at herself in this?*

As the examples indicate, questions are an important focusing tool for supervision. At the same time, supervisee questions challenge supervisors to respond in ways that are facilitative to both the process of supervision and to the supervisee. We believe that some questions merit direct answers, but most require facilitation of the supervisee's reflection.

Some Questions Merit Direct Answers

Such questions as the ones below illustrate the type of situation where the supervisor can give a direct answer.

> *How do I contact the State Licensing Board?*
> *Should I include the signed release of information in my subpoenaed materials?*

The supervisor has information that the supervisee needs and that can't be uncovered within the supervisee. A response such as, "Where might you go to find your answer?" can set up a situation that implies, "I know the answer; you don't, and I'm not going to tell you." This "cat-and-mouse" situation is not conducive to a relationship of equal respect. We suggest you give the answer and move on to more growth facilitative topics.

Some Questions Merit Responses to Facilitate a Supervisee's Reflection

Two situations arise that may influence supervisors' responses to supervisees' questions: supervisors know the answer; supervisors don't know the answer.

> *What else could I have done with this client?*

> *Was that okay? (referring to a clinical decision)*

> *The client wants to keep the door open for more air, but then confidentiality can't be assured. I know it's warm, but he can't be that hot. What should I do?*

In these situations you, the supervisor, have an answer for the supervisee. You have dealt successfully with these situations. You could just share your knowledge (also known as your pearls of wisdom). However, your answer may not be the answer that best fits the supervisee. We recommend you proceed in the same manner as though you did not know the answer, since in fact, you may or may not. By facilitating supervisees' process you allow them to grow in personal knowledge and self-efficacy. Examples of possible responses to the above situations are listed below:

> *I've seen you respond successfully to other clients in similar situations. What makes this situation different?*

> *What do you want to do?*

> *So somehow his response gets you stuck. What are you thinking and feeling when that happens?*

What part of this has you stuck—the client's response to you or your response to the client?

These responses facilitate supervisee reflection. Ultimately, there may come a time for supervisors to share ideas, but we are aware that our "pearls of wisdom" are needed far less often if we have facilitated the supervisee's reflection.

What to Do When Your Supervisee Persists in Seeking Praise

When supervisees are struggling with the incongruence between therapeutic practice and a usual way of responding in relationships, they may seek direction from a supervisor. Encouragement for working with the uncertainty of new learning is helpful. It acknowledges effort, notes progress, and allows the counselor to feel heard by the supervisor. On the other hand, praise is less growth producing. Praise is a positive judgment of a person or action that implies that there is a polar opposite requiring a negative evaluation. This black-and-white external evaluation can be instrumental in diminishing the thoughtful internal evaluation necessary for reflective practice.

Supervisees who seek praise from supervisors present an interesting paradox. Supervisors may wish to reinforce facilitative practice and yet be unsure of how to do this without the use of praise, which decreases internal reflection. We recognize that this tension in supervisors easily is diminished with a simple, "Great counseling!" and that this very response tells the supervisee nothing. Learning to acknowledge effort and to assist supervisees in self-reflection are two skills that can facilitate supervisee growth. This supervisor skill is demonstrated in the following interactions.

Supervisee: *How did you like the way I used the empty chair technique?*
Supervisor: *What was your observation of how it worked?*

*****

Supervisee: *How did you like the way I used the empty chair technique?*
Supervisor: *Sounds like you took the risk and tried something new.*

*****

Supervisee: *How did you like the way I used the empty chair technique?*
Supervisor (grinning): *Sounds like you'd like my evaluation. I'm interested in yours.*

All three examples go in different directions but focus back on the supervisee. The supervisor responses in turn encourage the supervisee to reflect on the process, acknowledge the behavior of risk taking, and reflect the meaning of the supervisee's question, turning it back to the supervisee with humor and softness. The result is supervisee self-reflection and evaluation, both invaluable processes for clinical practice. Supervisor praise may feel warm and comforting to the supervisee but has no value in enhancing supervisee growth.

What to Do When You, the Supervisor, Are Feeling Insecure

Beginning supervisors often find themselves experiencing feelings of insecurity. They may have adequate knowledge of therapeutic practice but suddenly are thrust into learning about supervision and becoming supervisors in a near simultaneous process. This sudden change may be complicated by additional factors such as the ones below.

- The supervisee is older than the supervisor.
- The supervisee has credentials from other fields commonly given higher status. Lawyers and physicians would fall into this category.
- The supervisee appears to have advanced therapeutic skills.
- The supervisee has many more years of experience in the field than the supervisor does.

A typical way of dealing with such feelings is to ignore them, taking the less risky route of avoidance. A second avenue would be to move towards a more genuine relationship, as illustrated in the following steps.

First Step

If you are reading this section, you probably already have taken the most important step toward action; your self-reflection has led to the recognition that you are feeling insecure. The second step is probably also in your grasp. Discuss your feelings with other students if you are in a supervision class or with your supervisor. Discussions can assist in the normalizing of this experience, since others probably are experiencing similar feelings.

Other Possible Interventions

One intervention is to bring this implicit dynamic to an explicit level. This is evident when supervisors choose to bring up thoughts and feelings in cultural discussions in which both supervisors and supervisees self-disclose about the relationship. One of us experienced such a dynamic when requested to supervise a psychiatrist. Supervisor self-disclosure was helpful in starting a two-way conversation that led to a shared destination of a supervisory/collaborative relationship. An example of this type of self-disclosure follows.

Here we are. You're a psychiatrist with a biological knowledge base that I don't have, and I'm a therapist with a knowledge base of practice that you don't have.

Frankly, I'm a bit intimidated by your knowledge. I'm wondering how this difference in backgrounds and occupations may be affecting you?

The result of such a discussion begins an immediate change in the relationship dynamic between supervisor and supervisee. They are no longer separate but are united in this area of exploration.

I recently shared this idea of mutual self-disclosure with a supervisee in a similar situation. She had not brought up the subject directly, but it had been implied in her discussion of a case. When I inquired about her thoughts around an interaction with a teacher, the insecurity emerged. "I could never do that," she replied. "I can't let her know my feelings. I need to pretend that I know all about this factor affecting my client. I'll have no credibility if she knows I am insecure." This new professional in the field perceived that an open discussion would bring even more insecure feelings. She did decide that preparing well by going over ideas in her mind would assist her in restoring balance to her feelings.

A second factor that was already helping was to talk about these feelings in supervision. The empowerment that comes from nonevaluative discussions in supervision was evident a month later when the supervisee reported that she had actually invited this open self-disclosure with the teacher. This had resulted in a facilitative and non-threatening discussion, which had enhanced both the teacher consultation and the supervisee's self-efficacy.

What to Do When Your Supervisee Says, "My Client...

- *Relapsed*
- *Quit Therapy*
- *Did Not Show up for a Scheduled Appointment*
- *Did Not Complete an Agreed Upon Contract*

...and It's All My Fault!"

Each of us in our role as counselor/therapist has been faced with the above situations many times. We have learned how to understand them and to respond without assuming responsibility for the client's behavior. Our supervisees, especially those with little or no experience, have learned neither the lessons of understanding nor responding. Their lack of experience often coupled with self-doubt, low self-confidence, and an inability to assess accurately factors that contribute to the appearance that therapy is not working, place supervisees at risk for focusing on themselves and making statements such as, "I did something to make this happen." Supervisees are prone to make broad assumptions about the dynamics of the situation and conclude that they are at fault. They seem unable to comprehend the complexity of many of these client situations, and overlook who or what may have influenced the client's decision.

Supervisors need to be prepared to work with and assist supervisees who are struggling to understand and accommodate the powerful emotions associated with self doubt, inadequacy, and fear of failure. Others needing assistance are those who doubt their own competency and compensate by assuming too much responsibility for the client. We have developed some ideas for working with supervisees who have taken on all the responsibility when the counseling/therapy has not been adequate.

Things to say:

- Challenge supervisees to develop alternate explanations for client decisions other than the supervisee is at fault. If the supervisee has difficulty doing this, you may want to provide some yourself.

  Explain how you came to the conclusion that you caused your client not to show up today.

- Challenge supervisees to examine their own internal messages, such as:
    o I can help every client.
    o If a client fails to change, I am not competent.
    o I can help clients regardless of their problems.
    o I can control my client's life.

  I notice you seem to have adopted an internal message, "...." Shall we explore this?

- Explore your supervisees' feelings of fear, inadequacy, self-doubt, and incompetence.

  Talk about your feelings after you found out your client's mother is a psychiatrist.

- Provide support through encouragement and focusing on their strengths and successes. Active support of supervisees has been most helpful to them in being able to disengage from their clients.

Comment: Our goal is to assist supervisees in disengaging from the external focus of client progress and move to an internal focus of their own work. Shifting to a more internal focus places less reliance on the client's progress and more reliance on the self-evaluation of the supervisee's growth. We view this cognitive restructuring as the key to supervisee change.

What to Do When You, the Supervisor, Are Attracted to a Supervisee

Although sexual intimacy between supervisor and supervisee is forbidden by ethical standards, sexual attraction is not. Attraction is a function of human nature and is a reality to be expected and managed. Supervisory relationships have many of the same characteristics as therapy relationships. The disclosure of personal concerns and intense emotions by the supervisee can create an environment conducive to attraction. Whether the attraction is individual or mutual, the supervisor has the responsibility to take whatever steps are necessary to deal with it in an ethical manner. The supervisor is in a position of power because of the professional role and therefore has the duty and obligation to maintain appropriate boundaries.

The ethics of this situation are clearly stated in every mental health professions' code of ethics. Rather than restate the obvious, we have put together two lists. The first contains a series of situations in which a heightened awareness of dual relationships, and attraction in particular, may be warranted. The second is a relatively short list of behaviors for supervisors in resolving issues related to attraction.

Situations to be watchful for:

- Supervisees and supervisors of a similar age
- Supervisees and supervisors with the same sexual orientation
- Shared interests and values between supervisees and supervisors
- Invitations for social interaction
- Attending the same courses, conferences, or social events
- Practicing in a rural area where professional distance would be difficult
- Supervisees who are vulnerable because they are new to an area, have few social supports, are leaving an intimate relationship
- Business arrangements between supervisee and supervisor
- Asking or being asked to keep an activity a secret
- Asking for or accepting a favor
- Feelings of physical attraction
- Transient feelings of sexual attraction
- Current partners seeking to supervise one another

When you sense sexual attraction:

- If it is from your supervisee, attend to it in some way. Discuss the attraction. A recommendation for therapy may be in order.
- If you are attracted to your supervisee, discuss this with your supervisor and/or consult with peers.
- After consultation, the end result may be to end the supervisee/supervisor relationship.
- Carefully document your supervision.
- Consult, consult, consult!

There are two messages in these lists. The first is not to act on the attraction that is felt. The second is to attend to the attraction in an active manner. This may include such activities as discussing it with your supervisee, bringing it to your supervisor, seeking consultation from your colleagues, or discussing it in group supervision. The bottom line is to not hold on to it but to share your responsibility with others and allow them to assist you. Not to attend to such a serious matter could easily result in personal and professional tragedy.

Section 3

SUPERVISION VIGNETTES
FOR EXAMINING CLINICAL PRACTICE

One way to examine clinical practice in supervision is to explore actual supervision case material. This section of the book consists of 17 vignettes taken from clinical practice. To assist in selection of a vignette for group discussion or individual reflection, we have identified topics as well as titles. All of the case illustrations in this account are based on practice. Names and other details have been changed. They are drawn from our work supervising university practicum students and from our supervision of clinicians in the field.

Mothers

Dr. Wilkins was the instructor/supervisor for a practicum section in individual counseling. During a supervision session late in the semester, Joan, a student counselor, was struggling with a client. Joan reported that the client was having a difficult time with her mother. The client said she felt her mother was not paying attention to her; in fact, she was feeling abandoned. Joan said she was not able to focus on her client's issue and that she could not see how the issue was a problem for her client. Dr. Wilkins noted that this was somewhat unusual behavior for Joan, who she had observed was a perceptive and insightful counselor.

In noting the anomaly, Dr. Wilkins remembered that in a previous discussion of cultural background, Joan had disclosed that she had been adopted as a baby and that during her college years she had made contact with her birth mother only to have been rebuffed by her. At that point, Dr. Wilkins asked Joan whether her client situation reminded her in any way of her own situation. Joan responded by saying, "No, my mother has been a wonderful support." Just as Joan was concluding, tears came streaming down her cheeks, and she said, "I have two moms." Joan later disclosed that the tears were an unconscious response, as they had come before she had made any conscious connection to her birth mother.

Group Exercise

Break into small groups and choose either the cultural background issue or the countertransference issue in this case as your group's focus. The exercise also may be used as an individual reflection.

1. Discuss ways counselors and supervisors may share their cultural backgrounds.

2. Which of your own values were identified by this story, and how may these values facilitate and/or reduce your effectiveness as a supervisor?

3. Can Joan be an effective counselor given her countertransference?

4. How would a supervisor decide when to confront supervisees with their countertransference, and what approach would be appropriate?

5. When supervisors experience a loss of objectivity or their emotions are triggered, where do they go for assistance?

I Just Want My Way

Supervisee: *I've just got a simple question. A few months ago my client's parent signed a release of information form for me to talk with the child's physician, which I did. Subsequently, one of the client's parents said I was never to talk with the physician again without checking with her first. Well, the child is going to see the physician next week, and I want to call the doctor and tell him how things have deteriorated and how the child really cannot control himself at times. I know the parents will say it is not okay, but I do have the signed release of information form. May I just do it and perhaps ask the physician not to say anything? Or the other thing I could do is call the parents, ask permission, and tell them that if they don't let me talk with the doctor, I'll need to report them to DHS for neglect of their child.*

You are the supervisor. What are some of the possible directions you can take with the supervisee? Place an X in front of the one you might choose first.

___ The exploration of ethical issues such as fidelity and justice

___ Confidentiality guidelines

___ The exploration of the legal mandates for abuse

___ What the supervisee is experiencing

Group Exercise

Explain your rationale for your choices. What might you say to the supervisee?

Comment: This scenario points out how a supervisor can have an issue that leads to a favored direction. For example, one supervisor may find that ethical issues take precedence, even when other directions may be more growth producing for the supervisee. Another supervisor may feel pulled towards legal issues or transference/countertransference. We want to be sure to get to the exploration of ethical and legal guidelines, but we would begin by focusing on the supervisee.

The Colorful Coat

A client arrived for her appointment, wearing a distinctive coat. The therapist remarked on the bright and beautiful colors. Twelve hours later, after a particularly long day, the therapist arrived home to find a box at her doorstep. Inside was a coat identical to the one her client had worn earlier in the day. The note inside relayed how far the client had traveled to find the coat, claiming it was worth it as a way of saying thank you for all the help the client had received.

The clinician is your supervisee. She states that when trying to return the gift to the client, the client became distraught and said she felt like this rejection was of her. The client asked the therapist to keep the coat at least until her next appointment, and if the therapist had not changed her mind by then, the client said she would take the coat back. The client went on to say that she could not return the coat because it was on sale.

1. What are some of the issues for the supervisee?

2. What are some of the issues for the supervisor?

3. How would you proceed in supervision?

4. What personal issues are triggered by this incident?

Talking

A number of years ago I was reviewing literature in cultural diversity for a workshop in clinical supervision. I came across an article entitled, "Homophobia in the Supervisory Relationship: An Invisible Intruder" by G. Russell and E. Greenhouse. It appeared in *Psychoanalytic Review* in February 1997, and was co-authored by a heterosexual supervisor and a lesbian supervisee. In reading the article, I was struck by the similarities between these two authors and myself and a current supervisee. Although they were accepting of their differences and felt comfortable with each other, they had never discussed their most obvious difference, sexual orientation. The main thrust of the article was the result of their discussion about sexual orientation.

I was intrigued and gave the article to my supervisee to read. At our next supervision session, she arrived with the article in her hand, saying, "We must talk about this right now!" We did, and what happened changed my way of addressing diversity. The simple act of talking about our differences led to the disclosure of information neither of us had consciously considered. More importantly, it led to a deeper understanding of one another and a greater sense of trust and respect.

I will never engage in another supervisory relationship without initiating a discussion about cultural background. Even though we think we know and understand one another, talking about differences brings out information and feelings that often may not be addressed. Both the supervisor and supervisee deserve time to share their cultural backgrounds, as doing so has the potential to make supervision more effective and satisfying.

1. What are some ways you address culture in your supervisory relationships?

2. What assumptions do you make about your supervisees' cultural backgrounds?

3. What cultural values, beliefs, and attitudes do you hold? Which of these would be important for you to share with your supervisees?

4. What are some ways a supervisor's cultural background may influence supervision?

5. What in your cultural background may influence your supervision?

Divided Loyalties

A counselor reports to her supervisor that she has decided to go against agency policy by not reporting a one-time heroin use by one of her clients. This is a private agency with clients who are prisoners of the state corrections department on work release and who have substance abuse problems. She explains that she likes the client and thinks he has a good chance to be successful after being released by the Department of Corrections.

The counselor explains that her client admitted to her while in therapy that he and his girlfriend had injected heroin the previous weekend. He said this was the only time he had taken any substances during his three-month work release program. His use had not been picked up on the mandatory drug test administered by the Department of Corrections. After admitting drug use to his counselor, he made a similar disclosure to his therapy group. The group members spoke out, urging the counselor not to report him if she expected to have any credibility with other clients in the agency.

Following the group therapy session, the counselor went to the agency director and asked her what the agency policy was concerning the disclosure of substance use during therapy. The director responded that the agency's policy required counselors to disclose any substance use by their clients to the Department of Corrections and that any use by individuals in the work release program would mean immediate incarceration.

The counselor explained her position to the supervisor by saying that she believed her primary responsibility was to the client. In addition, she stated that the Department of Corrections had its own testing program, and if it did not pick up her client's use, she did not feel a responsibility to do the department's work. Furthermore, she said she was concerned about her own credibility with clients in the agency and did not want to do anything to jeopardize it, since without it she would be ineffective, and a loss of credibility would likely cost her her job.

You are the counselor's supervisor.

1. In view of the fact that your supervisee has decided to go against agency policy, what is your responsibility?

2. Do you have a responsibility to make a report to the Department of Corrections? Explain your response.

3. How might federal laws governing confidentiality apply in this case? How might state law apply?

4. What direction would you take next with this counselor?

Silver Spoon

Your supervisee is working in community mental health. His clients are mostly street people, many of whom have been in prison. In addition, many have multiple mental health diagnoses, health problems, little or no income, and an absence of social support. Your supervisee's office is the street, and occasionally he does interviews in shelters and group homes. Your overall impression of him is that he is a very bright and talented young therapist.

The supervisee has provided you with the following background. His mother is a successful surgeon, and his father is a corporate lawyer. He grew up in an upper middle class community, was sent to private schools, and graduated from an Ivy League college. During his master's degree training, his internship was at a college counseling center. He described his growing up as privileged, and he did not want for anything. Furthermore, he said he wanted to work in the counseling field and with this street population because he thought he could make a difference.

This is your supervisee's first job, and you have been assigned to supervise him. His first few weeks were filled with enthusiasm and an eagerness to learn. Lately you have been observing comments such as, "I love working with these people, but I'm not sure they like me." "My clients take a lot from me and…." "My clients don't seem to be making changes no matter how hard I try."

1. What are the cultural implications you observe in this situation?

2. How would you approach your supervisee to assist him as he begins to struggle?

3. How do the cultural facts of this case relate to you and your cultural background?

4. In what ways does your cultural background influence how you would respond to this supervisee?

Contradictions

Counselor: *I am uncomfortable doing assessments outside the office.*

Supervisor: *How about in the office?*

Counselor: *I am fine; I'm comfortable.*

Supervisor: *What makes you uncomfortable doing field assessments?*

Counselor: *I'm scared.*

Supervisor: *Scared.*

Counselor: *Yeah, I'm scared when I have to go in a client's home.*

Supervisor: *Tell me more.*

Counselor: *Well, I just don't know these clients and how they will behave. I don't feel confident in predicting their behavior.*

Supervisor: *So when you see the same client in your environment, you are fine, but seeing that person in his or her own environment is uncomfortable for you.*

Counselor: *Yes.*

Supervisor: *Help me understand more about what happens when you do an assessment in the field. Give me a specific example.*

Counselor: *Well, just yesterday we went out to do an assessment of a woman in a group home. When we arrived, the staff gave us a private space for the interview. Right away she became agitated and at times incoherent. I have never worked with someone who is psychotic before.*

Supervisor: *I need to clarify something. Are you feeling physically unsafe when you are doing field assessments?*

Counselor: *Yes.*

Supervisor: *It sounds like you have another staff member with you when you do field visits.*

Counselor: *Oh yes; we are not allowed out by ourselves.*

Supervisor: *So you are feeling physically unsafe, and it sounds like you were feeling uneasy working with this woman who has a serious mental illness.*

Counselor: *Yeah. It was particularly disconcerting when she wouldn't look at me and showed a lot of anger.*

Supervisor: *Suppose this woman came to see you in your office in the agency. What would it be like seeing her there?*

Counselor: *I would be more comfortable. I could sit next to the door, and there would be staff around.*

1. What are the apparent contradictions you have observed in this situation?

2. How would you, as supervisor, conceptualize this situation?

3. How would you respond as supervisor?

4. When supervisees inform you that they feel unsafe, what ethical guidelines might influence your response?

5. Brainstorm different unsafe situations that supervisees may encounter, and explore possible supervisor responses.

6. Explore your own feelings that arise in situations in which supervisees report feeling unsafe.

Mother's Death

About 20 minutes into a supervision session, your supervisee stops and, with tears in his eyes, says, "As you know, my mother died two weeks ago, and I am having a difficult time with her loss. I am struggling at home, at work, and with my clients. I know you can't be my therapist, but can you provide me with 30 minutes of counseling? I think it would be very helpful in getting me past some of my sadness and the distraction it is causing me."

1. What are some of the possible responses to your supervisee?

2. Our codes of ethics are quite clear that supervisors cannot supervise and counsel the same person. Are you feeling a conflict in this situation? Discuss.

3. Discuss the legal and ethical concerns raised by this vignette and the following comment.

4. What unintended consequences of engaging in therapy with this supervisee do you perceive?

Comment: The facts in this situation indicate this is a one-time event, time limited, and there is awareness on the part of both parties as to what is being requested. In such situations, the supervisor may elect to engage in counseling on a one-time basis. This would be a rare exception, and boundaries would have to be clearly delineated. The one-time-only restriction may not be violated.

The Too-Ethical Supervisee

A counseling intern came to class and stated that her site supervisor had said she must call the state authorities and report the childhood sexual abuse of a 40-year-old man she was seeing in therapy. She was reluctant to do this, since (a) it had happened so long ago, and (b) the client had begged her not to tell because it could only hurt him in his job and with his family.

The intern asked the university supervisor what she should do, since she felt ethically bound to not report the incident. She believed doing so would be harmful to her client and would not accomplish anything positive. The university supervisor assisted the supervisee in exploring the issues. The following day the intern called the site supervisor and asked to discuss the matter further. She still had not reported the material to the authorities. She said she realized she might not graduate for defying a supervisor. She also stated she was ethically bound to not harm her client and therefore would not make a damaging report.

1. The supervisee recognizes that countertransference is present but does not connect that to the ethical decision of not reporting the abuse. She has carefully laid out a case for not reporting, using Kitchener's ethical decision-making model. You are the site supervisor. The supervisee is clearly at an impasse. What is your next move? Why?

2. You are the university supervisor. Discuss your thinking and any actions you might take.

3. What are the personal and professional issues for you that are triggered by this case?

4. Discuss the different responsibilities of a site supervisor and a university supervisor.

Nuts

The supervisee arrived blurting out the issue before she even sat down in the room.

I'm going nuts! In my new job I am supposed to go to this meeting every Wednesday from 9:00 to 12:00 with seven other players. Dr. Bruce is the staff psychiatrist, and she runs the meetings. Well, according to the printed agenda, the meetings are run by the director, but everyone defers to Dr. Bruce. She talks and talks and talks. Maybe that is the true meaning of filibuster. ARGHHHH. I hate it! One good thing did happen though. Being new on the job, I don't have anyone to really talk and process with or complain to about all that goes on. Well, after the meeting, the director called me to her office and asked what I thought about the meeting. I tried to be noncommittal, but I did say the discussion seemed a little one-sided. She said, "I guess!" and proceeded to talk in a slightly sarcastic way about "The Dr." I totally agreed with her, and it felt good that she confided in me, but on the other hand, I felt that was really unprofessional of her.

As the supervisee began this story, she was animated and entertaining with gestures and facial expressions that mimicked Dr. Bruce. My mind had strayed when Dr. Bruce's name was mentioned. I knew her well. What a bore! She delivers monologues and holds the rest of the world captive during them. I could share that I had worked with Dr. Bruce for a number of years and struggled similarly. My supervisee had just mentioned that when the director confided in her, it made her feel both welcomed into the inner circle and uncomfortable. I wanted to repeat the dynamic and give her my perception of Dr. Bruce.

1. As the supervisor, what feelings might you be experiencing in this situation?

2. What dynamics are present in this supervision session?

3. What do you do when you are caught up and siding with the supervisee's situations?

4. What would you say to the supervisee at this point?

Authoritarian Dad, Nurturing Mom

Following are two situations we have experienced as supervisors. How might you handle them? What would you say next? You may wish to role-play them to gain clarity.

Situation 1

Your male supervisee has a cultural background with elements from his southern rural early childhood, midwestern and eastern boarding school years, and adulthood in the eastern states. In class he works to please his professors, to be known by them, and to ask the opinion of everyone, allowing him to adjust to the system at hand. His first counseling experience in practicum is proving difficult. As you, the supervisor, listen to his counseling session tapes, you notice that he is silent to the point of discomfort. When you ask him about this, he replies, "Well, my client knows that I am the male and that it's up to me to make decisions for her. I am waiting for her to finish. I want to give her a chance to speak before I tell her what to do."

What will you say next? Why?

Situation 2

Your supervisee, a female, begins a supervision session as follows:

Supervisee: *Before we get started, I just want to tell you how helpful supervision always is for me.*

Supervisor: *What part is helpful?*

Supervisee: *Well, you don't judge me. That is the best. You know, I just wish I had had you for a mom. My mother was cold, icy, and always told me what a failure I was.* (Tears begin to roll down her cheeks.)

What will you say next? Why?

A few weeks later you are asked to evaluate this student's skills with an instrument that asks students to rate themselves on a continuum and explain their rating, using clinical examples. You, the supervisor, fill out the same form. When you and the supervisee share your evaluations, the student bursts into tears and says, "I should have known you would do this to me. You only looked at the bad things I did. I'm better than that. I can't imagine why you would do this to me. You really are just like my mom!"

What will you say next and why?

All Tied Up and No Place to Go

Your supervisee, a therapist with a community agency, has been working with a family for a year. She has known that an experienced psychologist visits with one of the children at home, where he also discusses parenting with the caregiver.

Yesterday when the supervisee arrived at the home, the psychologist was there alone with the child and suggested that they both work with the child together. He said he believed this would approximate a child being with two parents and having the undivided attention of both. The supervisee agreed, feeling both pressure due to the psychologist's senior professional status and reluctance because this was not a well-thought-out and planned intervention. She agreed to be a support to the child, mainly reflecting meaning and feelings of the child's actions and verbalizations. The psychologist said he would play a role similar to the father who had rejected the child and that the child would come to believe in his personal ability to work thorough such situations as a result of the nonjudgmental support of the supervisee. The supervisee found herself feeling more uneasy with this explanation. As the session with the child proceeded, the psychologist loosely tied up the child in such a way that the child was restrained. The supervisee took action and in her best therapeutic manner untied the child.

The supervisee reported that the child was visibly shaken and subdued by the session. The psychologist indicated that the supervisee should not have interfered, that the child was reexperiencing abuse at the hands of his father, and that this was a therapeutic moment. The supervisee disagreed, believing that the reenactment of trauma should never be done lightly, no matter what the therapist's theory was. The supervisee's operating theory was child-centered and did not allow for such therapist actions.

1. What is the dilemma your supervisee is facing?

2. What are some possible countertransference feelings or issues for the supervisee? How might the supervisor access these issues?

3. What countertransference issues were you experiencing as you read this?

4. What are some possible ways to proceed in supervision? What could you say to begin that journey?

5. What role might culture play in this dilemma? Explain.

Subsequent to supervision, the counselor goes to her agency supervisor to report the incident. The administrative supervisor says that Dr. Dollarhite is a Ph.D. and must know what he is doing. The supervisee returns to you, the clinical supervisor, and says, "What do I do now?" How do you respond?

Don't Ask, Don't Tell

You are the instructor/supervisor of a master's level practicum course. You receive a call from one of your counseling students, who sees children at a local elementary school. She reports that a fourth grade student just disclosed to her that her mother hit her with a stick. The counseling student observed welts on the girl's arms and hands and notified the school counselor immediately. The school counselor stated she would follow school policy and notify the principal. The instructor/supervisor directs the counseling student to check back with the school counselor and verify the disposition of the report to the principal.

Two days later at her weekly individual supervision session with the instructor/supervisor, the counseling student reports that she checked back with the school counselor and was told that the principal had decided not to call the state authorities, since he had reported the family before and nothing had happened.

1. As the practicum instructor/supervisor, what actions would you take in this situation?

2. How would you direct your student to act?

3. What does your state law direct you to do in situations like this?

4. What are the possible implications of bypassing the school authorities and making a report directly to the state?

5. How familiar are you with your state statute on mandatory reporting of abuse and neglect? Do you have a copy of the statute?

Suicide

You are the instructor/supervisor of a master's level practicum course, midway through the semester. During the weekly group supervision, a student counselor presents the following situation.

"I saw my adolescent client this morning at a local high school. He told me that he wants to kill himself. When I questioned him further, he said that he has access to a gun and a plan for killing himself."

When questioned further, the practicum student says that he tried to reach the school counselor, but she was in a meeting. He reports that he remained with the client for a short time. Prior to leaving for a meeting at another school, he directed the client to return to class.

The practicum student adds that the client's parents do not speak English. He also reports that he did not attempt to reach the school counselor later. He says he knew he had practicum class that afternoon and was certain he would get help on how to handle this situation.

1. As the practicum instructor/supervisor, what immediate actions would you take?

2. What would you say to the practicum student in question?

3. How would you respond to the other students in the practicum class?

4. What actions would you take to ensure that this type of incident did not happen again?

Wonderful Mom

Your supervisee is running a therapy group made up of women, all of whom are mothers. One of the group members often talks about her daughter. She has reported that her daughter is not doing well in school and that she is so angry she threw her daughter out of the house over the holidays. She has expressed resentment over ever having had this child, tallies the amount of money the daughter has cost her, and professes to be a wonderful mother whenever she is challenged by other group members. This mother's motto is, "Do it my way, or you are out."

Your supervisee states that she is "having all sorts of countertransference with this group member. I find myself frustrated and angry. I feel like I am up against a wall. This group member is making no movement, and I feel inadequate and ineffective."

1. What are some different ways of conceptualizing this case?

2. What additional information might you want to know about the supervisee?

3. How would you proceed with this supervisee?

4. What would you say next to the supervisee?

Appointment at 6:00?

Your conditionally licensed supervisee misses a scheduled bimonthly appointment. He calls you two days later and asks to reschedule. He reiterates that he was involved in a crisis at the earlier time and forgot to notify you of his unavailability. Two months go by during which he comes to all scheduled appointments. Once again he does not show up for an appointment or notify you. The following day he calls you with apologies for his forgetfulness. He mentions that it would be helpful if you would call and remind him a day ahead of appointments.

1. How would you conceptualize this situation?

2. What are some of the possible responses to the supervisee?

3. What is your personal reaction to not being notified prior to sessions?

4. If you were asked to respond to a licensure board inquiry concerning the supervisee's performance, how would you respond?

No Clothes

Your supervisee is a high school counselor who reports that she has a dilemma. Several teachers have come to her to say that they are concerned about a sophomore girl who wears as few clothes as the school policy allows and wears them in a highly provocative way. Furthermore, the teachers claim that her talk with the boys in class is highly sexualized.

Your supervisee states that she has spoken with this girl, who maintained that she was doing nothing wrong, did not have a problem, and did not want any help. In talking with the girl's mother, your supervisee observed a similar mode of dress, and although the mother was thankful for your supervisee's concern, she did not share those concerns. The supervisee comes to you expressing a great deal of frustration over the girl's behavior, as she feels it could cause serious problems for the girl in the future. In addition, she continues to receive feedback from teachers about the inappropriate nature of this girl's behavior, implying that your supervisee needs to do something about it. However, your supervisee continues to be told by both daughter and mother that this is not a problem for them.

1. List the critical elements of this case from a supervisee perspective.

2. What is your personal reaction to this situation?

3. How would you conceptualize this case?

4. What will you do to assist the supervisee in supervision?

5. How would you respond to this supervisee? What is the rationale for your response?

Section 4

TRAINING

Professional development and ongoing education and training have emerged as an ethical obligation (Bernard & Goodyear, 2004; Bradley & Ladany, 2001; Haynes, Corey, & Moulton, 2003; Stoltenberg, McNeill, & Delworth, 1998). Many mental health professional associations place a premium on staying abreast of the ever-changing developments in the profession by requiring hours of continuing education as part of recertification. No less is required of supervisors, many of whom have received little or no training in supervision. Most of these supervisors adopt the model they experienced in their own training. However, reliance on an informal method of supervision is no longer acceptable. After all, we would consider doing therapy without training to be unethical. It follows that supervising without training is unethical as well. We strongly believe that trained supervisors are essential for the continued development of efficacious practice.

The training curriculum that follows is one that we have taught over fifteen times in a quest to train all of the site supervisors that serve our students. We hope it assists you as you take on the responsibility of furthering professional competence.

Workshop in Clinical Supervision

This four-day workshop in clinical supervision was designed to meet the educational standards set forth in the approved clinical supervisor (ACS) credential established by the National Board of Certified Counselors. The workshop takes place over four days with a two-week-or-more break between the second and third days. Workshop participants are required to do homework over the break. They must make a 50-minute videotape with a supervisee, complete a written critique of that session, create a written supervisor disclosure statement, and read a series of articles and handouts, totaling 100+ pages. We estimate these assignments will take approximately 6 hours, which completes the workshop total of 30 hours.

The workshop experience provides participants with an opportunity to understand selected major theoretical models of supervision, tasks and functions of supervision, supervisor responsibilities, and to develop through practice individual supervision approaches. The overall goal of the workshop is to equip novice supervisors with foundational information and supervised practice as well as to provide experienced supervisors with additional knowledge and skills to enhance their current supervisory practices.

Day one includes a discussion of supervision and some background on supervision models, roles, and functions. We do two live demonstrations to model the supervisor behaviors we are teaching. In the second demonstration, we involve the participants by continually stopping the dialogue after one or two minutes and asking them how they would respond. We find that doing this generates considerable discussion, and participants are able to try out ideas with minimum risk. A discussion of this demonstration technique begins on page 37. At the end of the first day, we ask everyone to complete a 10-15 minute videotape of supervision of one of the other workshop participants. We explain that this tape is for their eyes only and ask them to review it at home that evening. We have received frequent feedback indicating, "If I knew I would have to make a videotape, I wouldn't have come." This has sensitized us to making this experience as comfortable as possible.

Day two begins with a discussion of legal and ethical issues facing clinical supervisors. The morning concludes with a second supervision taping session. We provide time for participants to review their tapes and to choose a segment on which they would like to receive supervision. After lunch there is a discussion of administration issues, followed by each participant presenting a segment of tape from the morning and asking for feedback. We end these two training days with instructions on the homework required over the break. As tapes are sent to us, we view them and write critiques. In addition, we pick out one segment from each person's tape to be played on the third day. We inform participants ahead of time that we will be choosing and playing tape segments as models of effective supervision for the rest of the group. We have found that participants are both comfortable and pleased to be recognized like this. In addition, this provides us with an opportunity to show models of excellent supervision to the entire group.

Day three begins with the replaying of tape segments, followed by a discussion of multicultural issues in supervision. In the afternoon, there is a brief presentation on supervision relationships, followed by the taping of a 20-30 minute supervision session. We ask everyone to take the tapes home, review them, and choose one segment for peer group supervision on day four.

Day four starts with a discussion and demonstration of a peer group supervision model. The model is fully explained beginning on page 60 of this book. Following a discussion of the model and a demonstration in which everyone participates, each participant has about 15 minutes to present his or her tape segment for supervision. We use the group supervision model we have just taught them earlier in the morning, allowing us to reinforce the group supervision model as well to give the group an opportunity to try its skills at providing feedback. We seldom intervene, because we believe the group gets more out of the exercise by finding its own way. There is a discussion on evaluation in the afternoon, followed by continued peer group supervision. We end in a traditional way by asking for verbal and written feedback.

Objectives

At the completion of the workshop participants will be able to:

1. State personal beliefs and assumptions about supervision
2. Define clinical supervision and describe its purposes and historical background
3. Describe the essential elements of a developmental model and the discrimination model of supervision
4. Describe supervisory roles and functions and how they are integrated into an effective supervisory relationship
5. Understand and apply the methods and techniques of clinical supervision
6. Understand and apply legal and ethical standards in supervision
7. Describe evaluation methods, including guidelines for providing feedback
8. Describe administrative functions, including planning and record keeping, of supervision
9. Compare and contrast various intervention formats, including individual, group, and peer supervision
10. Describe supervision from a multicultural perspective
11. Demonstrate knowledge and skill in clinical supervision
12. Use interventions appropriate to the counselor's developmental stage
13. Demonstrate the use of a variety of supervision roles and functions
14. Choose and implement skills and strategies that enhance the quality of the supervisory relationship

A detailed outline of the workshop and of the out-of-class assignments described above follows.

Topic Outline

Day One   __Time__

Introduction

Clinical Supervision Overview   1 hour

Live Demonstration and Discussion   1 hour

Clinical Supervision Models   1 hour
       Developmental Model (Stoltenberg, McNeill, & Delworth, 1998)
       Discrimination Model (Bernard, 1979)

Lunch

Supervisor Roles/Functions   .5 hour

Methods and Techniques in Clinical Supervision Live Interactive Demonstration	1 hour
Videotaping and Discussion (Videotapes will not be shown.)	1.5 hours

Day Two

Ethical and Legal Issues in Supervision	1.5 hours

Videotape Practice
    Individuals will be in groups of three or four. Each person will
    record a 10-15 minute supervision session with another participant.
    Observers will take notes to be used later in the critique.
	1.5 hours

Lunch	
Administrative Issues in Supervision	1 hour
Critique and Discussion of Morning Practice	2 hours

There is a minimum of a two-week break between days one and two and days three and four. Each participant will send to the instructors a supervision disclosure statement and a 45-minute videotape of a supervision session with a written summary. In addition, participants are expected to spend several hours reading/studying the handouts and other related materials. The combination of preparing the videotape, writing the supervision disclosure statement, and reading is designed to account for six hours of workshop time.

6 hours

Day Three

Return of Videotapes and Discussion	2 hours
Multicultural Issues in Supervision	1 hour
Lunch	
Supervisory Relationship Issues	1 hour

Videotape Practice
    Individuals will be in groups of three or four. Each participant
    will record a 20-30 minute supervision session.
	2 hours

Day Four

Peer Group Supervision—Discussion and Demonstration	1 hour
Peer Group Supervision	2 hours
Lunch	
Evaluation in Supervision	1 hour
Peer Group Supervision, Continued	2 hours
Wrap-up and Workshop Evaluation	

Total Workshop Time: 30 hours

Sample Assignment Handout

Videotape and Disclosure Statement Assignments

The videotape assignment of a 45-minute tape of you working as a supervisor with a supervisee is an integral part of the workshop. As much as possible, we would like you to integrate the information we have presented thus far at the workshop and to focus specifically on the handout related to the structure of supervision. Submit a written summary and critique of your session with the videotape that you return to us. The summary needs to be no more than a summary of objective statements of what happened in the session. Another way of looking at this is that you should consider the summary as a supervision case note.

In addition, we would like you to critique your performance as a supervisor on the tape. The format for the critique is to use the discrimination model to describe your supervisor roles. Discuss the various functions that were a focus of your supervision session, and describe the relationship between you and the supervisee. Finally, discuss the developmental level of the supervisee and supervisor. If there were ethical issues that were evident, make a special notation of these.

A second assignment is to develop a disclosure statement for clinical supervision. The disclosure statement should be one you would use in your current work setting. Follow the guidelines presented in the workshop and the handouts. In addition, please bring copies for each member of the class.

This videotape, summary, and critique are to be mailed by _____ or before. Please mail them to: _____. If you have any questions, please call or e-mail us.

References

Bernard, J. M. (1979). Supervisor training: A discrimination model. *Counselor Education & Supervision, 19,* 60-68.

Bernard, J. M., & Goodyear, R. K. (1998). *Fundamentals of clinical supervision* (2nd ed.). Boston: Allyn & Bacon.

Bernard, J. M., & Goodyear, R. K. (2004). *Fundamentals of clinical supervision* (3rd ed.). Boston: Allyn & Bacon.

Borders, L. D. (1991). A systematic approach to peer group supervision. *Journal of Counseling & Development, 69,* 248-252.

Bradley, L. J., & Ladany, N. (Eds.). (2001). *Counselor supervision: Principles, process, and practice* (3rd ed.). Philadelphia: Brunner-Routledge.

Falvey, J. E. (2002). *Managing clinical supervision: Ethical practice and legal risk management.* Pacific Grove, CA: Brooks Cole.

Gray, L. A., Ladany, N., Walker, J. A., & Ancis, J. R. (2001). Psychotherapy trainees' experience of counterproductive events in supervision. *Journal of Counseling Psychology, 40,* 371-383.

Haynes, R., Corey, G., & Moulton, P. (2003). *Clinical supervision in the helping professions: A practical guide.* Pacific Grove, CA: Brooks Cole.

Magnuson, S., Wilcoxon, S. A., & Norem, K. (2000). A profile of lousy supervision: Experienced counselors' perspectives. *Counselor Education & Supervision, 39,* 189-202.

Nelson, M. L., & Friedlander, M. L. (2001). A close look at conflictual supervisory relationships: The trainee's perspective. *Journal of Counseling Psychology, 48,* 384-395.

Russell, G., & Greenhouse, E. (1997). Homophobia in the supervisory relationship: An invisible intruder. *Psychoanalytic Review, 84,* 27-42.

Stoltenberg, C. D., McNeill, B., & Delworth, U. (1998). *IDM supervision: An integrated developmental model for supervising counselors and therapists.* San Francisco: Jossey-Bass.

Wilkins, P. (1995). A creative therapies model for the group supervision of counsellors. *British Journal of Guidance & Counselling, 23,* 245-258.

114   References

Subject Index

Training, 107–111

Videotape
    and disclosure statement assignment, 111
    as a training tool, 108

Workshop in Clinical Supervision
    description, 107–108
    objectives, 109
    topic outline, 109–111